NETWORK CENTRIC WARFARE
Coalition operations in the age of US military primacy

PAUL T. MITCHELL

ADELPHI PAPER 385

The International Institute for Strategic Studies

Arundel House | 13–15 Arundel Street | Temple Place | London | WC2R 3DX | UK

ADELPHI PAPER 385

First published December 2006 by **Routledge**
4 Park Square, Milton Park, Abingdon, Oxon, OX14 4RN

for **The International Institute for Strategic Studies**
Arundel House, 13–15 Arundel Street, Temple Place, London, WC2R 3DX, UK
www.iiss.org

Simultaneously published in the USA and Canada by **Routledge**
270 Madison Ave., New York, NY 10016

Routledge is an imprint of Taylor & Francis, an Informa Business

© 2006 The International Institute for Strategic Studies

DIRECTOR-GENERAL AND CHIEF EXECUTIVE John Chipman
EDITOR Tim Huxley
MANAGER FOR EDITORIAL SERVICES Ayse Abdullah
ASSISTANT EDITOR Jessica Delaney
COPY-EDITOR Matthew Foley
PRODUCTION John Buck
COVER IMAGE Canadian Department of National Defence

Printed and bound in Great Britain by Bell & Bain Ltd, Thornliebank, Glasgow

British Library Cataloguing in Publication Data
A catalogue record for this book is available from the British Library

Library of Congress Cataloguing in Publication Data

ISBN 978-0-415-42733-3
ISSN 0567-932X

Contents

GLOSSARY

BPS	Boundary Protection Services
CCEB	Coalition Communications and Electronics Board
CENTRIXS	Coalition Enterprise Regional Information Exchange Service
COWAN	Coalition Wide Area Network
CTI	Cryptological Transformation Initiative
CWID	Coalition Warfare Interoperability Demonstration
EU	European Union
GAO	General Accounting Office
GCCS	Global Command and Control System
GIG	Global Information Grid
GIG-BE	Global Information Grid Bandwidth Expansion
ICT	Information and Communication Technology
JV2010	*Joint Vision 2010*
LIO	Leadership Interdiction Operation
LPDs	Landing platform docks
MIC	Multinational Interoperability Council
NCES	Network Centric Enterprise Services
NCW	Network Centric Warfare
RIMPAC	Rim of the Pacific
RMA	Revolution in Military Affairs
ROE	Rules of engagement
SATCOMS	Satellite communications
SIPRNET	Secret Internet Protocol Router Network
TCS	Transformation Communications System
UCP	Unified Command Plan

INTRODUCTION

Network Centric Warfare (NCW) seems to offer the possibility of true integration between multinational military formations, in a manner rarely experienced in conflict. NCW burst onto the military scene in 1998 in a seminal article by the late Vice-Admiral Arthur Cebrowski and John Garstka, two individuals who would go on to have important roles in shaping how the US military thinks about the future at the Pentagon's erstwhile Office of Force Transformation.[1] At the time, NCW was simply the latest in a long line of ideas influencing military thinking, stretching back to antiquity. Since its appearance, however, it has become a master concept underlying the direction of America's military 'transformation'. NCW, or variations on its themes, has also been adopted by many other armed forces around the world. However, it is still a concept under much operational and doctrinal development; even at this point in the 'war on terror', much of the work on NCW remains speculative.

NCW is shaping not only how militaries operate, but just as importantly what they are operating with. Military systems that cannot be networked and cannot share information are no longer on the acquisition lists of most developed countries' armed forces. In many ways, the global spread of NCW resembles the ubiquity of the Microsoft Windows operating system. Furthermore, the relationship between NCW and modern military operations mimics the role Windows plays in shaping both computer systems and their associated software. Just as every operating system has a 'kernel' – a 'program that constitutes the central core of a computer operating system … [that] has complete control over everything that occurs in the system' – so the US Secure Internet Protocol Router Network (SIPRNET) forms the kernel of this new operating system by virtue of its status as the national network of the world's most important military power.[2]

The changes in warfare that NCW is creating seem likely to extend far beyond the operational military environment, potentially altering the strategic landscape. America's military superiority over every other state effectively means that it alone is capable of sustained military activity on a global scale; all other powers are limited to their own strategic neighbourhoods, or capable only of short bursts of global activity. This means that the political use of conventional military force will be shaped by American will; other states participating in US-led coalitions must be prepared to work in an interoperable fashion. The operational aspects of American military doctrine now have global strategic impact. Still, how and even more importantly when American military power is used will be an increasingly complicated matter. None of the other contemporary great powers seek to challenge the international status quo, nor are they pursuing military capabilities that would allow them to do so. Irrespective of their conservative orientations, the cross-cutting challenges and opportunities presented by globalisation mean that there is little likelihood of an emerging political consensus on action between them and America. In many cases, the US will stand alone in terms of decisions to intervene or not in the international sphere.

The theory of NCW will reinforce this unilateral drift. While the application of computer networks to military operations is primarily intended to increase the amount of operational freedom military commanders have at their disposal, the twin requirements to guard the security of a network's information and to ensure that it accurately represents situational reality will mean that strict control of information will be necessary. This will raise significant issues for the way coalitions share information among their members; ensuring the integrity of a network's information must come at the expense of releasing it within a coalition.

The limited ability to implement open networks in coalitions will be reinforced by the nature and management of coalitions themselves. Coalitions are largely about scarcity, in terms of either resources or political legitimacy. Scarcity is relieved through sharing influence over policy among coalition partners. The willingness to share influence, however, is a function of how dependent leaders are on their followers. In the age of US military primacy, then, influence will be restricted to very few partners.

The paper concludes with an examination of how networks affected naval operations in the Persian Gulf during 2002 and 2003 as conducted by America's Australian and Canadian coalition partners. This is a particularly important case study of the impact of NCW on coalition operations, for a number of reasons. Despite its important role in the Gulf, the UK was deliberately not considered as it represents a unique case by virtue of its very close relationship with the US, and the relative size of the British military commitments to the 'war on terror' compared with America's other partners. By contrast, the smaller powers of Canada and Australia provide a much better case. Their navies are roughly similar in size, technical capability and professionalism. They each share very similar professional relations with the US Navy, and both have a long history of naval cooperation stretching back to the Second World War. Each played a leadership role for the coalition within their geographical areas of responsibility in the Persian Gulf. Most importantly, however, Canada and Australia each pursued very different strategic policies with regard to Iraq in 2003. As such, the case study reveals the impact that strategic policy has on operational issues, especially in terms of how information is handled within America's overlapping coalitions.

While both Canada and Australia ably met the challenge of networked coalition operations, the specificity of the circumstances raises serious questions over the future of wider military cooperation with the United States. In the future, America may only be able to cooperate intensely on military matters with allies and security partners that not only possess the requisite capabilities, but are also trusted enough to share its information resources. Such partners are likely to be few and far between, and those that enjoy this status will not necessarily be available for every military contingency the US will face. In effect, NCW may be painting the US into a very secure digital corner.

CHAPTER ONE

US Military Primacy and the New Operating System

Two issues are playing dominant roles in shaping the current political landscape. Processes commonly referred to as 'globalisation' are affecting every area of the world through environmental modification, electronic communications, financial shifts, and the evolution of a worldwide civil society. Juxtaposed with this multi-dimensional globalisation is US military primacy. In 2004, the United States spent $466 billion on defence; the next largest spenders were China and Russia, at $65bn and $50bn respectively.[1] These twin developments, one generalised across the planet and the other specific to the US, will interact in complex ways as the world responds to US military primacy, and as an increasingly globalised environment compels political, economic, humanitarian and military engagement between states.

The conjunction of these two issues underlines the political applicability of US military power. This became apparent early on in the 'war on terror', when then US Secretary of Defense Donald Rumsfeld indicated that military imperatives would take precedence over diplomatic considerations in constructing a 'coalition of the willing'. According to Rumsfeld, the US must 'avoid trying so hard to persuade others to join a coalition that we compromise on our goals or jeopardise the command structure. Generally, the mission will determine the coalition; the coalition should not determine the mission'.[2] To an unprecedented degree, how the US conducts its future military operations will shape how others conduct theirs.[3] American doctrines seem set to dominate military operations in the same way that Microsoft's Windows operating system dominates computer programming.

American hegemony and military primacy

Military power is only one aspect of America's hegemonic position, and it is by no means always relevant. The greatest source of US strength is found in the ideological sway it holds over much of the world; its inherent 'soft power', as Joseph Nye characterises it. The United States exercises an ideational authority unlike that of any other state. Despite this ideational influence, the extent of American control over the global economy is open to question. Moreover, a rising tide of anti-Americanism is challenging American soft power. The status of American military power, however, is largely beyond question, both rhetorically and in practice.[4]

The basis of American military primacy has been described in terms of 'command of the commons'. The 'commons' are those areas over which there is no national jurisdiction (most obviously, the sea and outer space) and those areas where military control is difficult to enforce. These areas can be used by any actor possessing the requisite capability. But because of the ubiquity of America's military power, as opposed to the 'niche' and localised roles played by other states, the United States is able to exploit these areas more effectively in pursuing its military ends. More importantly, it may deny the commons to others. Wresting command of the commons from the US would require a generalised war, which is clearly currently beyond the capabilities of any other state. Command of the commons in its essence gives the US global agency, a privileged global ability to act. When the US confronts its enemies in their own specific areas of local control, they will already have been greatly weakened through diplomatic, economic and moral isolation, and through stand-off military strikes from air, space and the sea.[5]

Command of the commons is enhanced not simply through the comprehensive nature of American military might, but also through its capacity for a global approach to operations. No other state possesses a comparable worldwide network of military outposts in friendly states, which provide logistics support for operations distant from the US homeland. The wide-ranging exercises that US forces conduct with the armed forces of allies and security partners also enhance American familiarity with the operational characteristics of international military actors, and with diverse operating environments. Finally, no other state organises its military activities on a global basis, as the United States does in the form of its Unified Command Plan (UCP). The UCP enables the American military to 'develop responsive war plans that can generate significant combat power in far corners of the world on relatively short notice'.[6]

The globalised nature of American military power does not obviate the need for allies and other security partners, as every US National Security Strategy has pointed out.[7] Although some have challenged the notion of unipolarity on this basis, it is the case that the strong 'have more ways of coping' than weaker powers.[8] The point here is that, at present, America's overwhelming military power apparently provides it with options to structure the world that other states do not possess. In previous eras, this type of dominant power would have been of such concern to other states that it would have given rise to alliances, arms races, and outright political and military confrontation. There is speculation that the European Union (EU) may evolve as a potential counterweight to American hegemony, or that China will in time become a potential peer competitor. However, the fact that war between the major states is now largely 'unthinkable'[9] suggests that American power does not threaten the core interests of potential rivals in the way that the rise of Spanish, French, German or indeed Spartan power did in the past. Concern over America's power centres on more generalised unease about global issues confronting all states, such as climate change, religious extremism and cultural domination in all its varied forms. The nature of these challenges has limited reactions to the scope of US power to considerations of restraint and 'socialisation' in order to keep American behaviour within acceptable boundaries, much as one would deal with a friendly but unruly dog.[10] The issue for other nations is not wars of re-balancing, but how to engage American power: prodding it into action here, restraining it there. Thus, while the US seeks to shape the future of the world, other states seek reflexively to shape America's engagement with it. In the present global society of nations, everyone has their own 'special relationship' with the United States.

Allies and dominance

The public falling out in 2003 between the United States and some of its allies, particularly France and Germany, caused some to wonder whether American hegemony might be declining. Unlike in 1956, when the US was able to force France and Britain to back down over Suez, in the post-Cold War environment of 2003 Washington was unable to make its allies modify their policies. Indeed, as the dispute went on each side became more intransigent. 'What this shows', argued Christopher Layne, 'is that it is easier to be number one when there is a number two that threatens numbers three, four, and five, and so on. It also suggests that a hegemon so clearly defied is a hegemon on a downward arc.'[11]

Yet as the French historian Raymond Aron has noted of another hegemon's decline, 'a change from *Pax Britannica* to the *Pax Americana* did not involve a change of universe, and pride, rather than the soul itself, suffered'.[12] Aron's observation points to the surprising absence of competition between the United States and Britain as they exchanged roles in the twentieth century. But it also bears some relevance to the absence of military competition between America and its Cold War partners. One might point to the surprising process of military 'de-globalisation' that took place throughout the 1990s.[13] While American military spending fell somewhat in the early part of that decade, it has since recovered to the levels of the 1980s. At the same time, no state has responded in kind to American spending, and none has sought to challenge US dominance in key areas of military technology such as electronic warfare, intelligence and surveillance. No peer competitor, whether China or Europe, has emerged in the military realm since the end of the Cold War, and no state seems likely to challenge the US in the near future. Given the huge disparities in power between the US and China, massive increases in China's military budget would be necessary to develop the kind of power-projection capabilities the US currently enjoys. Furthermore, such enormous changes would take years to mature to the level of operational proficiency that the US currently exercises.

A neutered Europe 'unable to focus its latent military power',[14] comprised of states incapable of fighting among themselves, Layne argues, has long been the goal of American policy.[15] If this is so, then it is at odds with America's declaratory policy throughout the Cold War, and with its continued irritation with the lack of European burden-sharing since 1991. Still, the creation of a strategic environment dominated by American power has been part of US security policy since the end of the Cold War. In 1992, a draft copy of the still-classified *Defense Planning Guidance* was leaked to the *New York Times* and the *Washington Post*. As the *Post*'s Barton Gellman reported:

> The central strategy of the Pentagon framework is 'to establish and protect a new order' that accounts sufficiently for the interests of the advanced industrial nations to discourage them from challenging our leadership while at the same time maintaining a military dominance capable of deterring potential competitors from even aspiring to a larger regional or global role ... 'we will

retain the pre-eminent responsibility for addressing selectively the wrongs which threaten not only our interests but those of our allies or friends, or which could seriously unsettle international relations'.[16]

This was a first attempt at reformulating American security policy to take account of the changes accompanying the end of the Cold War. Some argue that it was based on an honest attempt to reassess the doctrines that would guide American action abroad, and what America could expect in terms of cooperation from partners no longer existentially threatened as they had been throughout the Cold War.[17] Gellman noted that the 1992 document was not a revolutionary departure from traditional American policy, which had sought to ensure that no one power dominated any key region, placing it in a position to alter the global balance of power.[18] And indeed, the leaked document did refer specifically to the necessary role of allies and coalition partners, noting their 'considerable promise' in assisting America to further its interests abroad.[19] Additionally, some have argued that the 1992 document was in keeping with 'American exceptionalism', the notion that the United States always uses power benevolently. Some have noted this aspect of America's 'myth of invincibility', arguing: 'According to this faith, American global power is limited by its own political scruples and humanitarian self-restraint'.[20] Despite this, the document barely conceals its scepticism that such cooperation would be easy to orchestrate, or would be there simply for the asking: instead of relying on its own system of alliances, the US 'should expect future coalitions to be *ad hoc* assemblies', and 'should be postured to act independently when collective action cannot be orchestrated'.[21]

The policy did not withstand the withering criticism directed at it from both the media and America's allies; the language of *Defense Planning Guidance* was altered to make it more acceptable, and it seemed to be relegated to the status of a footnote in US security policy. However, the emergence of George W. Bush's first *National Security Strategy* in the post-11 September 2001 environment strongly recalls the words of the discarded 1992 *Guidance*.[22] Shortly before its publication, Bush noted in his 2002 address to the graduating class at the US Military Academy at West Point that 'America has and intends to keep military strength beyond challenge – thereby making the destabilising arms races of other eras pointless'.[23] The undertones of 1992 in subsequent US strategic policy, and the participation of several personalities from the first Bush administration, including the original document's author, Paul

Wolfowitz (who became Deputy Secretary of Defense in 2001), linked the two policies.

It seems that the quest for military supremacy remained part of Pentagon policy post-1992,[24] as shown by the development of the concept of 'Full Spectrum Dominance' during the mid-1990s. First articulated in the 1995 document *Joint Vision 2010* (*JV2010*), Full Spectrum Dominance was supposed to enable the US 'to dominate the full range of military operations from humanitarian assistance, through peace operations, up to and into the highest intensity conflict'.[25] Here was the articulation of a policy that called for American pre-eminence across the full span of military operations, not just in traditional conventional force-on-force engagements. The goals of 1992's *Defense Planning Guidance* might officially have been renounced, but they persisted as the sub-text to the development of the US military's response to the Revolution in Military Affairs (RMA). This strategic approach to novel military technology and new forms of organisation is clearly apparent in the erstwhile Office of Force Transformation's definition of military transformation as:

> A process that shapes the changing nature of military competition and cooperation through new combinations and concepts, capabilities, people, and organisations that exploit our nation's advantages, protect against our asymmetric vulnerabilities to sustain our strategic position which helps underpin peace and stability in the world.[26]

It is worth recalling Wolfowitz's observations, in a 2000 edition of *The National Interest*, on America's remarkable success in forming coalitions. According to Wolfowitz, this had been achieved not by 'lecturing and posturing and demanding', but by:

> demonstrating that your friends will be protected and taken care of, that your enemies will be punished, and those who refuse to support you will live to regret having done so. It includes lessons about the difference between coalitions that are united by a common purpose, and collections of countries that are searching for the least common denominator and for easy ways out of a problem.[27]

In the same issue, Robert Kagan and William Kristol, commentators closely associated with the so-called neo-conservative movement, raised similar themes in their article, entitled 'The Present Danger':

Those alliances are a bulwark of American power and more important still, they constitute the heart of liberal democratic civilisation the US seeks to preserve and extend. Critics of a strategy of American pre-eminence sometimes claim that it is a call for unilateralism. It is not. The notion that the US could somehow 'go it alone' and maintain its pre-eminence without its allies is strategically misguided. It is also morally bankrupt.[28]

Of course, this was not the first time that spokesmen for a pre-eminent power expressed such sentiments. Nearly 2,500 years earlier, Pericles had extolled the exceptionalism of Athens and its generosity towards its allies:

> it is only the Athenians who, fearless of consequence, confer their benefits not from calculations of expediency but in the confidence of their liberality. In short, I say that as a city we are the school of Hellas; while I doubt if the world can produce a man, who where he has only himself to depend upon, is equal to so many emergencies, and graced by so happy a versatility as the Athenian. And this is no mere boast thrown out for the occasion, but plain matter of fact, is proved by the power of the state acquired by these habits.[29]

While we may debate the limits to and constraints on American power, pointing to loosened control over global shifts of capital, growing anti-Americanism or the potential rise of new 'balancing' powers like China or the EU, no actor shares the will and capacity to act globally that is at the heart of American military primacy. Given the absence of investment by other states and institutions in building their military capability, US military pre-eminence is likely to remain unchallenged, at least in the near term. This singular capacity to command the commons, to act militarily at a global level as opposed to every other power's limited niche or local capabilities, challenges the very nature and need for alliances despite the apologetic language inserted, *de rigueur*, in national security strategies. It is this capacity, possessed by a singular nation, that prompted Singaporean diplomat Kishore Mahbubani to call in 2005 for a 'new contract between America and the world':

> There needs to be an open and candid discussion, involving all sections of humanity, on the nature of the world order that will be realistically supported by America, the major powers, the weaker states, and the intelligent human community.[30]

It is a plea that can only be termed reasonable in the context of the vast disparity of power enjoyed by a single state compared with the rest of the world. However, the nature of globalisation and the risks it entails for all states ensure that enough common ground on which to base such a contract is unlikely to emerge quickly.

Globalisation, security and risk

Some have portrayed the split between the United States and the Franco-German axis in 2003 as a strategic sea change.[31] Of course, NATO has often been on the brink of crisis, whether over basic strategy, nuclear weapons, *Ostpolitik*, or burden-sharing.[32] The parting of company between erstwhile friends in this instance occurred over issues located far from Europe, and points to the changing nature of the transatlantic partnership, confronted by the challenges of failed states, nuclear proliferation and global terrorism. If unity on direct threats to national existence was hard to achieve, what hope can there be for unity over less immediate and more geographically distant issues?

The very nature of globalisation points to a complex future wherein insecurity is inextricably bound up with the promise of progress. The complex web of interdependent and cross-cutting relationships that make up globalisation not only renders its precise definition difficult, but also leads to considerable uncertainty in terms of its overall long-term social, political and economic effects.[33] Globalisation is inherently political in its tendency to produce both winners and losers depending on the nature of this complex interplay of variables. As each globalised relationship will produce variable outcomes for every participant, it is impossible blandly to characterise the overall process as either 'good' or 'bad', 'stabilising' or 'divisive'. As such, globalisation is by its nature ambiguous, and thus a source of insecurity even as it generates opportunities; it is at once enabling and disempowering.[34]

Globalisation gives unstable regions strategic impact far beyond their local areas. Such 'zones of war' produce 'leaking misery' in the form of terrorism, crime and refugees (both political and economic) heading for 'zones of peace'.[35] The result is intervention in failed states involving operations between paramilitaries, conventional forces and NGOs, undertaking a variety of operations including nation-building, humanitarian assistance, counter-insurgency, indigenous force training and outright combat – what the US Marine Corps describes as a 'Three Block War'.[36] In sum, globalisation produces an inherently complex security landscape defying any single solution around which international agreement can easily crystallise. This will mobilise politically a multiplicity of interests stretching across these zones of peace and war, further complicating efforts to find common ground.

An explicit example of the cross-cutting nature of globalisation is found in the role of global communications. The ability of ordinary individuals to inform themselves on international issues has contributed to the emergence of a 'global citizenry', capable of monitoring state action and insisting on the application of universalised ethical norms to any state's policy.[37] However, the same technology also permits those less committed to universalised notions of human identity to exploit differences in forms of justice, and to provoke violence between communities. The globalised riots and demonstrations against the negative portrayal of the Prophet Mohammed in cartoons in an obscure Danish newspaper in early 2006 point to the fragmenting effects that global communications may have.

As Lawrence Freedman has noted, 'a world in which threats are real enough but do not come from other Great Powers is bound to ask different questions of an alliance than one which is focussed on deterring or fighting a major war'.[38] The questions that will be asked of any partnership of powers will revolve around the uneven sharing of risks between these powers. What is striking about this condition is the necessarily subjective context in which consideration of potential policy alternatives takes place. The uneven nature of risk implies highly contextualised and individualistic definitions of what constitutes the 'correct' course of action. Modern democratic societies, politically mobilised by considerations of peace and war, are particularly prone to such debates given the 'risk' that military operations represent.

The question of risk as a fundamental aspect of modern society has been discussed extensively within sociological literature.[39] The notion of a 'risk society' emerges from the critique of the idea of progress. The notion of reflexive modernisation is the process by which society recognises that there is a price to be paid for all progress – that all actions have unintended consequences, whose nature often cannot be anticipated in advance. Because all actions carry the price of uncertain outcomes, risk assessments come to dominate all decisions regarding what action should be undertaken.[40] As Anthony Giddens reminds us, the notion of risk has always been present in human society in relation to natural forces that unfold in unforeseen ways. As our ability to shape our own environment developed, however, modern society began to encounter 'manufactured risks': man-made hazards as threatening as any in the natural world.[41] The nature of 'modern' society is to try to foresee and thus control the future consequences of human action. However, the consequences of nuclear disasters, climate change, the global spread of disease and invasive flora and fauna facilitated by modern transport, financial collapse precipitated by electronic currency speculation, and the effects of emerging technologies such as genetic engineering and nano-technology are so great and widespread as to be largely beyond the control of any single individual, group, organisation or state.

Risk defines itself in terms of its unpredictability and the uncertainty of cause and effect, thus removing it from the rational realm of scientific determination: one can speak only of probabilities.[42] Furthermore, these risks 'can no longer be limited to certain localities or groups but rather exhibit a tendency to globalisation which spans production and reproduction as much as national borders and in this sense brings into being supra-national and non-class specific global hazards with a new type of social and political dynamism'.[43] This dynamism is increased in the context of assessments of the probabilities of hazard as defined by the opinions of 'experts'; such 'social dependency on institutions that are alien/obscure/ inaccessible to those affected raises issues of trust and credibility'.[44] As risk is uncertain, it is inevitably politicised because of the varying impact it has on various social interests, each deploying its own experts and spokespersons. Therefore, the 'existence and distribution of risks and hazards are mediated on principle through argument'.[45] In its nature, risk is, therefore, socially constructed and articulated by the values and interests of those perceiving the risk.[46] The uncertainty that surrounds risk politicises it in terms of 'cover-ups' and 'scare-mongering'.[47] Debates over terrorism and weapons of mass destruction, both pre- and post-11 September 2001, have exhibited both of these characteristics.

Harvard political scientist Michael Ignatieff inadvertently uses the language of the risk society when he speaks of the inevitable 'political and moral debris' that accompanies all military action.[48] Indeed, war is the 'ultimate' in risk management:

> Air strikes are vulnerable to the vagaries of the weather, incorrect intelligence and the malfunction of sophisticated computers and guidance systems. Air crews might make errors of judgement under applicable rules of engagement, especially if they are engaged by the adversary's air defence weapons. As demonstrated in Kosovo, there can be accidents and mistakes even when targeting has been subject to meticulous planning and careful consideration.[49]

War, of course, is a highly politicised phenomenon, particularly within democratic societies, which must be convinced of the appropriateness of military action before sanctioning it. In these societies, risk assessment is nowhere more evident than when multinational military action is contemplated. In such circumstances, debate over war is not simply polarised, but also 'globalised'. The question of just how much of a threat Saddam Hussein represented to international peace and order in 2002–03 was largely framed within the context of a global debate on risk. The legions of pre-war assessments conducted by state intelligence agencies, international bodies and NGOs, together with phalanxes of informed experts on all sides of the question, was as much an orchestrated campaign as the military one that followed. That so many well-informed analyses later turned out to be so incorrect illustrates the subjectivity of risk assessments in relation to war.

Power and discourse among nations

Globalised debates on the correct course of action are nothing new to the field of International Relations. It is essentially engaged in an 'unending search for an understanding of the relationship between order and justice',[50] but is particularly challenged by conflict between different social and political ideals. Thus, the balance between order and justice is a timeless and discursive process. The end of the Cold War made this deliberation all the more pressing, as well as more difficult. The emergence of 'human security' as a focal point for international action, the rise of environmental concerns, and the empowerment of new voices attending the process of globalisation, whether in terms of debate over 'fair trade' or jihadist critiques of Western modernity, all added to what was already a complex agenda for establishing international social justice. But the end of the Cold War also gave rise, initially at least, to the hope that some solution might be found in terms of a 'New World Order' among the 'Free World' and newly democratised nations in an embedded liberalist epistemological community. This collective order of democratic states sharing common human values was ultimately unable to achieve unanimity on many issues of 'governance'. This should have come as no surprise: if, as Freedman suggests, 'strategy is the art of creating power',[51] then any strategy contingent on collective action must necessarily prioritise compromise as a key enabling condition of that strategy. Compromise, however, often implies suboptimal results, shown particularly by the lack of action over Darfur, and the nearly botched NATO operation against Serbia in 1999. The fading of the optimism that had initially greeted the end of the Cold War is thus more representative of the enduring 'clash of moral, national, and religious loyalties' reflecting 'the plurality of values by which all political arrangements and notions of the good life are to be judged'.[52]

Despite the pressure for action in Darfur, a resolution of that crisis seems as remote as ever – even in the face of numbers of killed, wounded and displaced many times larger than those affected by the attacks of 11 September 2001. Calls for action have been met with more diplomatic posturing by even those most supportive of such policies. Certainly, this points to the fact that human security as a practical priority was an illusion nurtured in the euphoria that accompanied the end of the Cold War. The plain reluctance of developed states to place their troops at risk in support of humanitarian missions indicates the hollowness of the values supposedly underlying their commitments to human security.[53]

The comparison between action on Iraq and inaction on Darfur reveals just how hollow this supposed commitment is. In each case, the United States has played an important leadership role. With Darfur, the US has gone so far as to label what is happening there as genocide, in the hopes of shaming other states into action, and establishing a legal and normative basis for intervention. However, where the US was seemingly willing to conduct Iraq operations unilaterally if necessary, an intervention force for Darfur remains stalled at the diplomatic level, and whatever funding is available is clearly far less than America is willing to spend in Iraq.[54] Europe, too, bears considerable blame in this matter. Where it was defiantly unwilling to intervene in Iraq, on human security issues supposedly more in keeping with Europe's ideological *Weltanschaung*, it has soft pedalled its reluctance to intervene in Darfur. Nor have the crowds across Western Europe, so opposed to war in Iraq, materialised to demand action in Darfur.

Inaction in this case has more to do with hard-edged compromises to political principles than any moral failing. The discursive nature of strategic decision-making, especially when those decisions are shared among many partners, requires a complex mixture of cooperation, confrontation, and competition in the process of hammering out the compromises of policy details. 'Interdependence of decision making means that effective strategy is based on the relationships involved and the opportunities it provides the various actors. It is necessary to anticipate the choices faced by others and the way your action shapes those choices.'[55] Naturally, compromise is an important currency in political relations, even in highly adversarial circumstances. The credibility of action can suffer if too much compromise is made, thus undermining the objectives sought. Strategic compromise may ultimately result in compromised operations.

As Ignatieff points out, in Kosovo Slobodan Milosevic took on military forces greatly superior to those he himself wielded, and nearly won.[56] In that conflict, Milosevic enjoyed the advantage of being a unitary actor confronted by a complex coalition of states only loosely held together by a broadly defined common objective. NATO fought under considerable constraints, which Yugoslav forces did not share. Intense political pressure was applied to minimise casualties (friendly, enemy and civilian) and attacks on civil infrastructure, and rapidly to halt ethnic cleansing.[57] The tensions between NATO's wartime objectives were a product of the tangled negotiations that ultimately brought the alliance to the first use of force in its long history. Potential Russian and Chinese vetoes meant that no Security Council mandate was in place, nor was NATO able to agree on a single legal basis for the war, with each member state applying various legal and political justifications. The UN itself was placed in a difficult situation: it wanted to see Kosovars protected from Serbian attack, yet at the same time needed to protect its authority in establishing the legitimate use of force according to the Charter. Kofi Annan, the UN secretary-general, was ultimately forced to split hairs, noting that 'it is indeed tragic that diplomacy has failed but there are times when the use of force may be legitimate in the pursuit of peace'.[58] Political compromises extended into the cockpit, where complex choices were faced between the need to protect pilots by flying at high altitudes, above the range of all but the largest Yugoslav air-defence weapons, and the need to protect civilians from inadvertent air strikes by flying much lower so that pilots could properly identify their targets.[59]

Finally, there were differences in how NATO partners interpreted the laws of armed conflict. States that had ratified the Geneva Conventions of 1977 interpreted Protocol One, prohibiting 'excessive' civilian casualties, as 'treaty law', setting a very high standard of practice that meant virtually any civilian casualty was excessive. The US had signed the Geneva Convention but had not ratified it, and thus interpreted Protocol One as 'international customary law' determined by the benchmark of how the United States has traditionally conducted air operations. This permitted a much looser standard with regard to what constituted excessive civilian casualties. The operational impact of this intra-alliance conflict of interpretations meant that some targets were off-limits, not only to specific nations but also to NATO in general. In practice, this generated two separate Air Tasking Orders, one for the alliance and a second for the US alone.

These differing interpretations of what constitutes 'excessive' recall the issue of risk discussed above. Excessive casualties are a 'risk' of any air operation, and place states and pilots not only in moral, but also legal, hazard. However, like risk, the definition of 'excessive' is socially constructed, and not strictly resolvable objectively. How it is defined will depend on a complex grouping of factors, including culture, history, national psyche and military doctrine.[60] Unpredictable elements, such as public opinion, will also play a significant role. Publics under direct threat will obviously define 'excessive' in different ways than those who are disconnected from the impact of war.

In standardising and regulating international behaviour, the expectation is that law, especially in combination with high-precision weaponry, will reduce, if not eliminate, the moral and political hazard of engaging in risky interventions. However, as has been shown repeatedly in military operations throughout the 1990s, the fact that Western forces may hold their actions accountable to high legal standards does not mean that their opponents will do so.[61] The use of hostages to deter military strikes or to lower public morale is increasingly common on the modern battlefield, as are strikes against civilians as proxies for military targets, thus increasing the political and moral complexity of military responses.

Power is a requisite for action, and if strategy is the art of creating power, then compromise and cooperation are ultimately important aspects of it. As Freedman continues, however, power is a relative concept, existing only as it is recognised by others, whether that recognition devolves from simple authority or brute force. Mastery over 'wilful beings', even in purely cooperative environments, involves the explicit exercise of power in all its guises. However, the greater the complexity of the social structure over which one is attempting to exert control, the more difficult that control becomes.[62] Kosovo illustrates this well. In attempting to apply seemingly straightforward and universal values, the result was an intricate mish-mash of conflicting strategic priorities and rules of engagement that ultimately placed greater operational constraints on the superior military force than on the outmatched Yugoslavs.

Primacy, risk and dominance: the new operating system

To recall Mahbubani's appeal for a new contract between America and the world, the challenge of globalisation and the opportunities and hazards it presents to all states suggests that, while such a call may sound reasonable, it is unlikely to be heeded. Even when partners share close moral and social values, as within NATO, achieving common purpose in that most risky of international endeavours, military intervention, has largely proved elusive. Currently, no great power seeks to alter the structure of the international system fundamentally. Indeed, even former revolutionary powers such as China and Russia desire greater integration with international society, for instance through membership of the World Trade Organisation. The absence of competition has led not only to a global failure to invest in military capabilities that would challenge American military predominance, but also to the absence of capabilities that would permit alternatives to American-led military interventions.

Articulating power ultimately involves engaging in risky behaviour, whether through the development of science and technology or by applying force. The subjective nature of risk ensures that how it is defined, especially if it is a risk to values and norms as opposed to specific interests, will remain highly contentious. Just as it has been difficult to arrive at common definitions of justice and order in the present international environment, the intricate interplay of domestic forces will ensure that each state regards the risks it faces in highly contingent (and ultimately expedient) ways, frustrating common action. The contested and politicised nature of risk and the discursive formulation of collaborative power suggest that struggles between America and its partners during crises will be contests over how best to 'spin' the available information.

In reality, the international environment will often not wait for diplomatic conversations to play themselves out, and will present a succession of crises for states to deal with. The conjunction of globalised opportunities and hazards, strategic indecision and US global agency through its military primacy prioritises American military operational methods. For the present, the command of the commons that the US enjoys ensures that only America has the capacity to act on a sustained, global basis. Thus, how the US defines risk will be the most important determinant for international action. Certainly, America's partners, and for that matter its adversaries too, will play important roles in the articulation of that risk. But because America's principal partners are all status quo powers,[63] they will seek to restrain it, rather than prod it into action, for fear of the possible strategic consequences for themselves.

For America, the key question may be how long to wait before acting. When it does move, the mission will decide the coalition. The Windows analogy that introduced this chapter is persuasive on a number of levels. In the current strategic environment, US military operational methods will structure the manner in which nations engage militarily, in the same way that Windows structures the global software environment. Local solutions, such as Israeli developments in urban operations or British ones in low-intensity warfare, are always possible. Where these are useful, America is likely to incorporate them into its own doctrine, just as Microsoft acquires smaller software companies to add value to its own suite of services.[64] However, nations seeking to participate in international military ventures will ultimately be forced to accommodate the American operational technique in the same way that software developers have had to get to grips with Windows. The next chapter discusses the nature of America's military operating system, and how it will interface with coalitions in this new environment.

CHAPTER TWO

Freedom and Control: Networks in Military Environments

> As we prepare for the future, we must think differently and develop the kinds of forces and capabilities that can adapt quickly to new challenges and to unexpected circumstances. We must transform not only the capabilities at our disposal, but also the way we think, the way we train, the way we execute, and the way we fight.
>
> Donald Rumsfeld, 2003[1]

Claims to the establishment of revolutionary ideas are difficult to verify in the present: only the passage of time can truly confirm the impact an idea will have on history. For example, immediately after the Second World War, nuclear weapons were widely believed to have revolutionised war. Nevertheless, their role in warfare has to date been latent, rather than direct. Secondly, as Colin Gray points out, the concept of a 'revolution in military affairs' is essentially an interpretation placed on the unfolding of events, as opposed to an objectively verifiable occurrence with a time and place attached to it.[2]

Much is also unclear about current developments in military networks. As in the case of nuclear weapons, it may ultimately prove impossible to implement information technologies militarily in the manner predicted by NCW's early proponents. Moreover, non-US militaries may devise alternative approaches to the use of NCW,[3] just as the combined use of armoured forces, wireless communication and aircraft took much trial and error by various powers before and during the Second World War.[4]

There is much that is promisingly novel about the military role that Information and Communication Technologies (ICT) might play. But while this might, from some perspectives, warrant the label 'revolutionary', at the heart of NCW lies a basic dialectical tension. NCW promises faster, more precise, more decisive operations thanks to information-sharing. In this regard, NCW is oriented towards increasing the operational freedom of choice for military commanders such that they can avoid or efficiently surmount the barriers that war creates through the enemy's active resistance, as well as the ignorance that the danger and chaos of operations generate. At the same time, because military operations are ultimately undertaken to ensure the security of the state, the military context is an environment of strict control and direction. The lethality of warfare further accentuates the critical nature of this operational dimension. Information is too critical to be unregulated, and its security is paramount. These two aspects – freedom and control, sharing and security – circle each other warily within the nature of NCW. If too much operational freedom is delegated to subordinate units, control is lost to commanders; if too much control is retained, operational flexibility is compromised.

Networks challenge the traditional hierarchical structure of military organisation; in the same manner, they also raise important questions regarding coalitions and how they will operate. Coalitions are centrally concerned with sharing – resources, influence, and information – and thus should be open to the use of networks. However, while a central premise of the information age is the power generated through information-sharing, networks can also be exclusive. US military primacy privileges America's own national secret level network, the SIPRNET, over other nations' smaller ones. On the internet, information has no borders; in military networks, however, it is absolutely essential that unbreakable frontiers are in place.

The origins of NCW

NCW is a relatively new concept, first appearing in the open literature in Cebrowski and Garstka's 1998 article, published in the US Naval Institute's *Proceedings*.[5] However, the idea of networking information among naval platforms began to emerge during the Second World War. The challenge presented to surface ships by aircraft, ubiquitous at sea for the first time with the appearance of modern aircraft carriers, required considerably more coordination among fighting platforms than had traditional naval gunnery.[6] The coordination of diverse vessels and missions resulted in the development of modern Combat Information Centres, or Operations

Rooms.[7] Contemporary tactical data-exchange systems such as Link and the Global Command and Control System (GCCS) can also trace their origins to the Second World War.[8] Finally, cybernetic theory, which forms the basis for much thinking on information and control, was developed initially as an off-shoot of ballistics research into the problems of anti-aircraft weaponry.[9]

After 1945, both the US Navy and Air Force continued to develop the role of information in the conduct of war; by the end of the 1970s, the US Army had joined them in this. Information has always been crucial to naval strategy, as navigation and locating the enemy are central to all naval battle. However, the US Navy's Maritime Strategy of the 1980s specifically exploited information-based technologies such as *Aegis* and advanced sonar to threaten the Soviet Union's coastline, thus potentially globalising any struggle over Western Europe.[10] Likewise, air and space technologies emerged at a steady pace after the Second World War, including advanced airborne radars, command and control systems, precision-guided munitions, stealth aircraft and satellite imaging.[11] Finally, the US Army's growing interest in operational warfare doctrines after the end of the Vietnam War led to concepts such as AirLand Battle. These required significant intelligence and the exchange of information between Army and Air Force units in order to coordinate deep strikes into Soviet rear areas.[12] After 1945 then, and with increasing intensity from the mid-1970s, each service independently pursued strategies with similar themes relating to the growing importance of information, and its transmission and sharing. This serendipitous evolution was noticed by the Soviet armed forces in the 1970s, and the issue of an American 'military technical revolution' was discussed in their professional journals.[13]

In some respects, the close of the Cold War marked the end of a political era, as well as a military one. The development of doctrines like the Maritime Strategy and AirLand Battle all pointed to the geographic expansion of the battlefield to something beyond what had been well understood, to that point, by 'operational art'. Operational art first appeared during the military changes of the early nineteenth century, when the enlargement of the battlefield, its growing complexity due to the rapid introduction of new technologies, and the growing role of the state's economic power in fielding and sustaining military forces led both to longer military campaigns and to theatre-scale warfare.[14] Aside from a solid grounding in tactics, successful military commanders needed to come to terms with the time and space dimensions of moving numerous large and complex military formations to achieve the ends of strategy. In the eyes of many strategic analysts, operational art reached its acme at the end of the First World War.[15] Former British Brigadier and historian of the First World War Jonathan Bailey makes the bold assertion that:

> Three-dimensional conflict was so revolutionary that the tumultuous development of armor and air power in 1939–45 and the advent of the information age in the decades that followed amounted to no more than complementary and incremental improvements upon the conceptual model laid down in 1917–1918.[16]

The operations projected by the US military at the close of the Cold War were inherently global in nature, however. Dealing with the complexity of this battlefield was beyond the individual competency of any single service, a point recognised by the introduction of the terms 'battlespace' and 'warfighter' in the 1990s.[17] Just as business was dealing with the challenges of an enlarging global market by exploiting ICT, so too the US armed forces were dealing with operational challenges on a similar scale, and exploiting the same sort of technology. By the mid-1990s, the US military was putting these new developments into doctrinal perspective.

The emergence of the concept

In 1996, Admiral William A. Owens published his article 'The Emerging System of Systems' in the National Defense University's journal *Strategic Forum*. This described a concatenation of sensors, command and control systems, and precision weaponry that would, he argued, result in 'dominant battlespace knowledge'.[18] In the same year, *JV2010* appeared, describing the 'conceptual template ... for achieving dominance across the range of military operations through the application of new operational concepts'. *JV2010* introduced the concepts of Dominant Manoeuvre, Precision Engagement, Focused Logistics and Full Spectrum Protection to achieve 'massed effects'. *JV2010* represented the distillation of 20 years of technological advance and operationally focused thinking in the US armed forces. Yet it was clear that 'information superiority' was the basis for these novel operational concepts. To that extent, they amounted essentially to a more elaborate restatement of the 1980s-era AirLand Battle ideas. *JV2010* incorporated conceptual advances in manoeuvre and joint warfare, but operations were fundamentally derivative of what had gone before. While *JV2010* spoke of the emergence of the RMA, a further step was required before one could begin to call these developments truly revolutionary.

The elaboration of NCW

Following Cebrowski and Garstka's seminal article, NCW was elaborated in three semi-official publications: *Network Centric Warfare: Developing and Leveraging Information Superiority*, written jointly by Garstka, Director of Research and Strategic Planning for the Office of the Undersecretary of Defense David S. Alberts and retired US Army Colonel Frederick P. Stein, published in 1999; *Understanding Information Age Warfare*, by Alberts, Garstka, Richard E. Hayes and David A. Signori, published in 2001; and *Power to the Edge: Command and Control in the Information Age*, by Alberts and Hayes, which was published in 2003.[19] Together, these three works form the canon from which most thinking on NCW has developed. Through a series of business case studies, *Network Centric Warfare* introduces the idea that networks generate power through the distribution of information. *Understanding Information Age Warfare* takes the idea of NCW and develops a theory about how information, knowledge and awareness interact in a military environment. *Power to the Edge*, a more conceptual piece, ruminates on the implications of information and networks for military organisations and their operations.

In exploring how computer networks are altering the economic and business activities of US corporations, *Network Centric Warfare* shows its descent from earlier works by Alvin and Heidi Toffler, who suggested in their influential *War and Anti-war* that 'the way we make wealth is ... the way we make war'.[20] Corporations, having linked together 'knowledgeable entities' (sub-units within the organisation) through computer networks, can take advantage of the shared awareness thus generated to make decisions faster and more efficiently, and to improve the accuracy of business predictions. Networked businesses may also improve collaboration between sub-units, and may ultimately create efficiencies in their supply chains and customer relations. *Network Centric Warfare* suggested that the compression of time and space caused by this shift would also impact on warfare. In essence, the same processes so important to creating better business decisions would also enable military commanders to create a condition of 'information superiority', analogous to earlier concepts of air superiority or sea control.[21]

Such capabilities would be increasingly important because of the growing complexity of the modern battlefield.[22] This new approach would produce a series of remarkable outcomes changing the very nature of warfare. Networks would permit the generation of combat power from highly dispersed yet agile military units because of their enhanced situational awareness. The authors of *Network Centric Warfare* argued that both the 'fog of war' and friction in military operations, while not eliminated completely, would be dramatically reduced.[23] As enhanced awareness would reduce risk, the cost of operations would decline, just as networks permitted businesses to reduce their costs.[24] The combination of these assets would permit networked militaries to create 'mass effects', instead of massing forces.[25]

In *Understanding Information Age Warfare*, these ideas are fleshed out into a full theory of operations. The authors begin with a series of assumptions about how experience ultimately translates into awareness, from which they derive a theory of warfare in networked environments. They suggest that we should consider the manner in which we obtain information about the external environment through the interaction of a set of logical assumptions. Sensory impressions of the environment can be directly experienced (seeing an event occur, for example) or indirectly inferred (through the interpretation of data from a sensor such as a radar). These impressions are then translated into 'information' by putting them into a 'meaningful social context' by identifying patterns through a comparison made between the sensed data and what is already known about the environment. These patterns represent 'knowledge', and comparisons between what is 'known' about the world (prior knowledge) and what is currently being sensed generates 'awareness'. Finally, with sufficient levels of knowledge, by identifying developing patterns the observer can draw inferences about what is likely to happen. In this way, awareness permits the observer to identify what is known about the past and present, while 'understanding' allows identification of 'what the situation is becoming'. At the end of this sensing process, the observer is capable of deciding what to do, and then acting on that decision. The whole process is similar to the famous 'OODA' (Observe, Orient, Decide, Act) loop developed by Colonel John Boyd.[26]

Alberts and his colleagues describe the world in which this process of sensing and interpreting data takes place as a series of interconnected 'domains'. Three principal ones are posited. The 'Physical Domain' is described as the scene where all action takes place. It is the location where military forces manoeuvre, strike and defend themselves, and action, being directly observable here, can be measured through direct and indirect sensing. The 'Information Domain' is where information is created, manipulated and shared. It is a virtual environment in which data is transferred and shared among actors through technology and software; at its heart, it is a medium for communication. The 'Cognitive Domain' resides in the minds of the actors participating in the network. In this domain, understanding is created through the interpretation of the data being communicated from the physical domain through the information domain. It is in the cognitive domain that information is evaluated and judged, and decisions made.[27] To these three domains, *Power to the Edge* adds a fourth, the 'Social Domain', which mediates the evaluations, judgements and decisions developed in the cognitive domain.

As Alberts and his co-authors point out, NCW is principally about sharing information and awareness.[28] It thus enables the development of superior awareness that ultimately translates into information superiority. This is described as the 'NCW Value Chain', which was first elaborated in *Network Centric Warfare* (as shown in Figure 1).

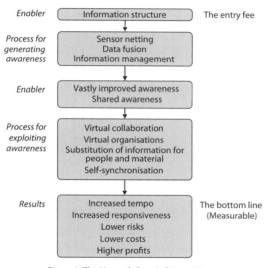

Figure 1. The Network Centric Enterprise

Adapted from Alberts, Garstka and Stein, *Network Centric Warfare*, p. 36

Figure 1 shows the series of inferences that lead ultimately to the establishment of increased combat power. By lowering the costs and risks associated with military operations, greater effects can be generated. Essentially, then, as the 'Tenets of Network Centric Warfare' assert:

> a robustly networked force improves information sharing and collaboration, which enhances the quality of information and shared situational awareness. This enables further collaboration and self-synchronisation and improves sustainability and speed of command, which ultimately result in dramatically increased mission effectiveness.[29]

Shared knowledge is critical for forces participating in a networked operation.[30] The end result of this sharing of information and awareness is the creation of additional combat power by enhancing the utility of information provided to decision-makers. Information can be characterised by its richness (or its quality) and its reach (or its ability to permeate every area on the network). Typically, the richer the information, the less reach it has. This is most obviously the case with classified information, which is generally closely held by those with a 'need to know'. However, those in the field with proper clearances may be unable to access this information because of their distance from those who control it. Lower-level information will spread much further through a network than the most highly classified material.

In a functioning network-centric environment, however, rich information no longer faces barriers to its reach. Those with the proper credentials in the field will be able to access even highly classified information in real time, thereby generating additional combat power.[31] A 'common operating picture' permits greater unity of command and purpose and de-conflicted missions, avoids duplication of effort, enhances early warning (and thus greater force protection), and allows resources to be used more economically.[32]

The requirements are, however, high. In the physical domain, all elements of a military force must be connected together, 'achieving secure and seamless connectivity and interoperability'. In the information domain, people and platforms must be able to access, share and, most importantly, *protect* information 'to a degree that [they] can establish and maintain an information advantage over an adversary'. Finally, in the cognitive domain, forces must be able to use this shared information to develop awareness of their environment, and share that awareness with other network participants. Unless these objectives are accomplished, military forces will be unable to 'self-synchronise', and thereby take advantage of the benefits conferred by the network.[33]

While it is the combined effect of the four domains that allows shared awareness and self-synchronisation, the lynchpin of the whole enterprise is the *security* of the information domain. Establishment of a combat advantage depends on information superiority, but this superiority must be protected. As *Understanding Information Age Warfare* puts it: 'in the all-important battle for information superiority, the information domain is ground zero'.[34]

With a theory in place describing the relationships between information, knowledge and awareness, further thinking concerned the implications for military operations in this new environment. The conclusions of this research emerged in 2003 in *Power to the Edge*. Here, Alberts and Hayes argued that, in order to take advantage of the opportunities offered by NCW, militaries would have to 'focus on C2, where information is translated into actionable knowledge'. In the modern battlespace, traditional procedures and organisations for the command and control of military forces would be unable to cope with the complexity that these forces will face. Alberts and Hayes argued that militaries had so far been able to adapt by using 'work-around' procedures that were typically unique to the time and place of a specific operation. Relying on these inefficient information-sharing practices in the face of the growing complexity of the modern battlespace will eventually frustrate the application of military power. Decision-makers in these challenging global arenas cannot possibly anticipate every outcome, nor do they possess complete knowledge about the environment in which they will operate. In order to maximise the potential offered by information, modern organisations must be capable of sharing their specific situational awareness with others.[35] Furthermore, since they cannot know who they will work with or which systems may be relevant, a high degree of agility would be necessary 'in terms of who participates as well as who plays what roles'.[36]

Given these observations on the demands of the modern military environment, the centralisation of command and control is increasingly impractical. Instead, power needs to be devolved to 'edge entities':

> Power to the Edge involves the empowerment of individuals at the edge of an organisation (where an organisation interacts with its operating environment to have an impact or effect in that environment) or, in the case of systems, edge devices. Empowerment involves expanding access to information and the elimination of unnecessary constraints.[37]

This vision is potentially revolutionary: in terms of its organisational and procedural implications, it strikes directly at the hierarchical structures that militaries have always relied on for command and control. It remains to be seen whether militaries will be capable of adapting to such a wide-ranging vision. Nevertheless, to illustrate the Pentagon's commitment to it, Alberts and Hayes point to the development of the Global Information Grid (GIG), which will integrate communications and computer systems into a secure, seamless 'infostructure providing access to a variety of information sources and information management resources'.[38]

The emergence of the GIG: networks and global military operations

The introduction of the GIG as a fundamental structural component of America's defences[39] points to the role of information technologies in transforming modern societies. Comparisons are easy to make between the military GIG and the civilian internet. Transformation itself seems to be guided by an 'internet paradigm' in terms of its overall vision.[40] In testimony before the US House of Representatives Armed Services Committee in 2004, Assistant Secretary of Defense for Networks and Information Integration John Stenbit described the GIG as a 'private world wide web' that would 'support the transformation of our warfighting and business practices'.[41]

Under current plans, the GIG will establish its core capabilities by 2010, at a cost of $21bn. However, full implementation is not expected until 2020. By then, the GIG will 'integrate all [Department of Defense] information systems, service applications, and data into one seamless and reliable network'.[42] Structurally, the GIG will be realised through four related endeavours: the Global Information Grid Bandwidth Expansion (GIG-BE),[43] the Transformation Communications System (TCS),[44] Network Centric Enterprise Services (NCES)[45] and the Cryptological Transformational Initiative (CTI).

Some analysts have speculated that such 'super networks' are inevitable.[46] Several features of modern operations contribute to this impression. The steady expansion of the operational battlespace since the eighteenth century and the globalisation of American defence tasks have demanded greater coordination among armed services. Missions such as close air support, the suppression of enemy air defences, missile defence and deep-strike operations all require close coordination among highly disparate force elements, many of them crossing service boundaries, some traversing traditional theatre and command boundaries. In order to accomplish missions such as these, even de-confliction of effort requires a high degree of communication and coordination between participating units. To go the next step and ensure effective joint coordination demands highly integrated planning.[47] Moreover, the human, economic, political and social costs of sending US forces abroad are increasing. Moving information instead of troops allows administrative, logistical, intelligence and other support to remain in the US, even during periods of combat.[48] Even the force providers themselves may not need to deploy in the massive fashion of traditional combat operations, relying on the speed, agility and manoeuvrability brought about by rapid and ubiquitous information sharing.[49] Finally, the importance of building stability in regions of civil war and social breakdown has helped to generate the complex battlefield identified by former Commandant of the Marine Corps General Victor Krulak as the 'Three Block War'.[50]

The highly complex nature of these shifts in the military environment prevents any one commander or organisation from possessing complete awareness of all critical aspects affecting operations. Geographically dispersed and organisationally complex operations, which may involve relatively small forces by traditional standards, require extensive information sharing. Networks assist in the planning and conduct of operations in many ways. Instantaneous communications have both shrunk the world, and accelerated decision-making.[51]

In this complex environment for the US armed forces, the very malleability of networks is also attractive. Information-age sociologist Manuel Castells has pointed out that 'nodes' on a network vary in terms of their overall relevance. The importance of any given node on the network stems not from its function or features, but from its ability to contribute to the goals established by the network. Nodes can be added or deleted from network architectures as their importance changes, or as the missions alter. This permits considerable flexibility (in determining the paths along which information can be sent), scalability (in terms of the growth or contraction of the architecture), and survivability,[52] allowing easy access to information 'anytime, anyplace, with attendant security'.[53] If fully realised, 'perhaps the single most transformational and operationally significant attribute presented by the GIG vision will be that US servicemen and women "at the edge" will no longer be at the mercy of someone remote from the fight determining what information they need'.[54]

Just as information superiority formed the base on which *JV2010*'s advanced concepts rested, *information sharing* forms the base on which the edifice of military transformation rests.[55] Information sharing is often conflated with intelligence sharing. Intelligence sharing is an important aspect of information sharing; however, it is only a subset of it. Information includes not just intelligence, but also sensor information, planning information and situational awareness. The 'fog of war' is commonly blamed for the waste of lives and resources associated with battle, and the failure of forces to achieve their purposes; the authors of *Network Centric Warfare* assert that any such fog is largely caused by a lack of battlespace awareness stemming from the inadequate distribution of information. Confusion stems from 'our inability to tap into our collective knowledge or the ability to assemble existing information, reconcile differences, and construct a common picture'.[56] While *Transformation Planning Guidance* blandly defines transformation in highly general terms,[57] the transformation necessary to overcome the fog of war and to achieve the vision portrayed above revolves around 'seamless' information sharing.[58] As *Network Centric Warfare* points out, information superiority is 'in part gained by information operations that protect our ability to collect, process, and disseminate an uninterrupted flow of information while exploiting and/or denying an adversary the ability to do the same'.[59] Ultimately, the ability to build a *collective* awareness upon the *collected* and limited awareness of platforms and individuals operating in the battlespace constitutes the basis of America's military transformation plans.[60] In the words of one USAF officer '[Internet Protocol] brings global connectivity to the kill chain'.[61]

Information vulnerabilities

This powerful vision for warfighting contains within it a significant vulnerability. The same technology that enables dispersed and small formations to magnify their operational power through information sharing also enables an adversary both to read the intentions and plans of a military force, and to alter the information to accomplish a variety of ends. The problems of unauthorised access to information sites that are supposed to be confidential are so widely understood as to have infiltrated popular culture; similarly, we are increasingly familiar with the threat posed by identity fraud, if not specifically in terms of national security. The threats of information denial and the clandestine alteration of stored data are less commonly appreciated, though just as damaging.[62] With the exception of a 'denial of service' attack, all of these methods involve penetrations of secure systems. Identity fraud is the digital equivalent of introducing a 'mole' into a supposedly secure organisation. The damage that 'malicious insiders' can cause to information systems points to a fundamental change in the nature of warfare. Traditionally, defence has always been the stronger form of warfare, but relations between offence and defence are reversed in terms of information security. As a study by the National Academy of Sciences described it:

> Imagine a situation in which truck bombers in a red truck attempt entry to a military base. The bomb is discovered and they are turned away at the front gate, but allowed to go away in peace to refine their attack. They return later that day with a bomb in a yellow truck, are again turned away and again go away in peace to refine their attack. They return still later with a stolen military truck. This time the bomb is undetected, they

penetrate the defenses and they succeed in their attack. A base commander taking this approach to security would be justly criticised and held accountable for the penetration.[63]

The difficulty of establishing identity in a digital environment[64] highlights the danger such penetrations pose to the security and integrity of an information environment.

A second challenge to information security on the GIG comes from authorised users of the system, who might compromise information from simple ignorance. In its essence, digital information is persistent and transportable: it is easily copied, archived and shared. The implications for inadvertent disclosure and subsequent propagation of classified information are evident. The Google search engine routinely archives all information it categorises, permitting users to view material that has since disappeared from the web pages on which it was originally placed. The same miniaturisation developments that have enabled electronic communications have also eased the problem of transporting large amounts of data over distance. Networks permit the rapid replication and translocation of information in ways that, in the past, spies could only dream of.[65]

Control versus anarchy: the problem of information assurance

These essential issues of information vulnerability have not gone unnoticed by US security agencies. Nevertheless, there has been no fundamental progress on information assurance, in contrast to the rapid developments in communication links and information sharing since the 1990s. In the 1990s, according to the US Government Accounting Office (GAO), the Defense Information Assurance Program, although it made limited progress, ultimately failed to meet its goals.[66] In 2004, the GAO identified three issues posing particular challenges for the GIG: deciding when and how much information should be posted; establishing rules to ensure that the GIG could work securely without compromising the benefits of flexible and dynamic information sharing; and convincing data owners of the value of sharing data with a broader audience and trusting the network sufficiently to post it. All three point to the critical role played by information security.[67]

The GIG's development programme subsumes the CTI, a $4.8bn project funded by the National Security Agency and involving the development of advanced firewalls, multilevel security protection, and High-Assurance IP encryptors.[68] Any information assurance system, however, has to accomplish a variety of goals. As defined by the US Department of Defense, information assurance is:

> information operations that protect, and defend information and information systems by ensuring their availability, integrity, authentication, confidentiality, and non-repudiation [which] … includes providing for the restoration of information systems by incorporating protection, detection, and reaction capabilities.[69]

In accomplishing these tasks, however, the systems engineer confronts the essential nature of digital information. Examining the sub-concepts embedded within the above definition of information assurance, 'availability' of information is for 'authorised' users only; 'integrity' of information means protection from 'unauthorised' change; 'authentication' involves verifying the identity of the originator of a request for/author of data; 'confidentiality' involves ensuring data from 'unauthorised' disclosure; and finally, 'non-repudiation' involves incontrovertible proof of the identities of those using information on a network.[70] Each of these aspects relates either to the fundamental authority, or control, over how and whether network data is to be stored, shared and manipulated, or to the identification of participants using such data. In sum, the challenge of ensuring security casts a large shadow over digital collaboration in military environments. Control of information in terms of both its security and its proper interpretation is of paramount importance.[71]

These requirements[72] suggest a fundamentally different orientation to information compared with the events that led to the emergence of the internet. Indeed, the control necessary to guard against even a single point of failure in information security suggests elements of a police state where 'every node is a sensor that can relate security information to those tasked with securing the network'.[73] This vision of near-totalitarian control of information clashes with the anarchic nature of the internet itself.

In contrast to the highly controlled military networks, no single authority controls the internet. It is an 'anarchical society' in the same sense that Hedley Bull described the international environment.[74] Just as in international relations, the absence of authority does not preclude a degree of order: the technical protocols for the transmission and sharing of information (TCP/IP and HTML and its variants) for example. While legal regimes are being established, in a global communications environment they depend largely on self-interested enforcement and compliance in a manner similar to international law. Still, there is enough order to permit the global conduct of a considerable amount of industry and business in this anarchical electronic environment.

In the same manner that concepts of justice are internationally contested, so the internet is also anarchical in terms of how truth is understood. There are no gate-keeping features on the internet.[75] Websites like Wikipedia take advantage of this aspect, as well as the dynamic, malleable nature of digital information.[76] The popularity of 'blogs' and their growing influence on news reporting within the media is a similar issue. The ability of sites like the 'Drudge Report' to unearth key political scandals in Washington relies on differing approaches to how truth is mediated between blogs and traditional news organisations. The commitment to professional standards of reporting by mainstream publications like the *Washington Post* ensured that rumours of an affair between White House interns and the president were unpublishable without iron-clad sources. Likewise, there is widespread academic criticism of Wikipedia.[77] In effect, the web becomes a location for debate over truth owing to the multiplicity of sites presenting differing slices of reality, permitting web-surfers to arrive at their own unique conclusions. The effect of this is, of course, the development of sub-communities convinced of 11 September 2001 conspiracies, or American possession of UFO technology at its base in Groom Lake ('Area 51').[78] Irrespective of these charges, the interpretation of truth on the internet is similar to how abstract terms such as justice and freedom are interpreted in the international environment: each of these problematiques owe their origin to the anarchical setting in which they are situated.[79]

That the internet should display these anarchical features is not entirely surprising, according to Castells. In his analysis of what he calls the 'Network Society', its emergence was influenced by three key features, including the culture of individual freedom inculcated on American campuses and in the counter-culture movements of the 1960s. The peace movement, the civil-rights struggle, and the growth of environmentalism during this period were founded on the defence of civil liberties, the advancement of free speech, and opposition to traditional sources of authority. Similarly, the academic culture of universities, especially in the United States, encouraged shared discovery, where professional communication was the basis for academic progress and the advancement of truth. Each of these movements 'stood in sharp contrast to the world of corporations and governmental bureaucracies that had made secrecy and intellectual property rights the source of power and wealth'.[80]

Pekka Himanen asserts that the information sharing on which the 'network society' and its electronic sinews are based has permitted the establishment of a 'culture of innovation', sometimes referred to controversially as the 'hacker ethic'.[81] The spirit of this culture is one of innovation, individuality and networking. It approaches work as a child does play, and emphasises the value of creation over the spirit of the profit motive. 'Money centredness leads to the closing off of information. Innovation lives on the open flow of information'.[82] This orientation towards information, freedom and innovation has also inspired technological movements such as the Open Source Initiative and the associated development of the Linux Operating System.[83] The free exchange of information has undoubtedly formed the basis of the explosion of technological and scientific advances of the late twentieth century. Whether militaries can take advantage of the innovation that stems from such sharing will depend on their willingness to compromise the strict information security protocols that impede such sharing.

The fundamental dialectical tension within the network-centric vision

This necessarily limited discussion of the role of information and networks in modern military thinking, and the development of the GIG emerging from the nature of NCW as contrasted with the development of the internet and its impact on modern society, suggests the tensions that underlie these developments. On the one hand, we can note that information exchange within military contexts has a long history and hardly constitutes a revolutionary development. What does seem to be revolutionary is the near-instantaneous global sharing of information permitted by developments in ICTs. The potential offered by these technological developments seems to suggest new approaches to how time and space function in military operations, and reflects changes in fundamental principles such as mass and concentration.

The power that militaries may derive from networks comes at the price of ensuring the security of the information domain from direct attack or clandestine infiltration. The complexity of this mission in a digital environment, where concrete identities are difficult to establish, suggests the need for a level of control over information that contrasts starkly with the nature of networks in civilian society. In effect, the military use of ICTs seeks to exploit their capacity for innovation, creativity and the expansion of knowledge. At the same time, however, the level of control that networked militaries require to protect the operational advantages of networks entail risks that obviate the beneficial features that were sought in the first place.

This risk may be exaggerated.[84] The Open Source Movement accepts the positive role that trade secrets play in some product development, where the competitive advantage generated through research and development must be protected against competitors.[85] Similarly, an examination of the principles that underlie the Open Source Movement and, indeed, Hinamen's culture of innovation call to mind the military principle of *Auftragstaktik*.[86] Control and restraint have featured strongly in the architecture of the internet. Control through information is central to the notion of cybernetics,[87] and there is plenty of literature[88] on the Orwellian nature of databases and the centralised control of information in government and society. Nor do digital insurgents necessarily enjoy greater technological advantages over GIG users due to their ability to manipulate data freely within the anarchical environment of the internet: the dialectic between innovation and control will play itself out in both the civil and military domains of the network environment, and will do so in unpredictable ways.

Networks enhance power through their scalability, survivability and flexibility. The ability of actors to take advantage of these features, however, depends on 'the pattern of power present in the [structure] of the network'.[89] As Cebrowski observed, if 'you are not on the net … you are not in a position to derive power from the information age'.[90] But just as not everyone on the planet is able to access the internet, so not all states' military forces are able to interoperate effectively with those of the United States. In many studies, this has been blamed on inadequate capital investment in ICTs, or on a failure of US technological developments to facilitate high levels of allied interoperability. This focus on a growing 'digital divide' misses the point that fragmentation is a structural feature of networks; as Castells puts it, networks 'search for valuable additions everywhere in order to incorporate them, while bypassing and excluding those territories, activities, and people that have little or no value for the performance of the tasks assigned to the network'.[91] This results in a differentiation between those who are sources of innovation, those who simply carry out instructions, and those who are irrelevant as either workers or consumers.[92]

The role that coalition partners will play in shaping the larger network and the goals towards which it will work will not necessarily be determined by technical capability or the ability to 'interoperate'. While 'plug-and-play' interoperability will undoubtedly be important for coalition partners, who is allowed within the larger confines of the network, and the role that they play once they are there, will be determined by the political value they bring to any endeavour, as established by very traditional national interests. In most coalition operations, the SIPRNET will be the most important network, and so America will establish the policies under which data will be shared between coalition partners. Questions must be posed as to whether coalition partners can also play roles as inno-vators within a network, or whether they will be relegated to less powerful roles, drones in other words. The term 'flags around the table' heard frequently in the context of coalition operations, neatly captures the reality of partners as politically valuable but militarily irrelevant players. And so we return to the issues of freedom and control. For all the latitude digital information provides, a strict logic constrains its users. Even as it offers greater operational freedom for military commanders, information assur-ance limits freedom of action. Even in the most liberal of national security networks, information assurance guarantees that coalition interoperability will be subject to an extraordinarily high degree of control. If unfettered trust is difficult to establish in a purely national setting,[93] then its achieve-ment in a multinational military network is most unlikely, even between the closest of allies.

CHAPTER THREE

International Anarchy and Military Cooperation

While capable of mounting large, rapid and decisive operations to achieve certain limited ends, the United States remains tied to its allies to assist it in maintaining international order: as technologically advanced and well funded as the US military is, it simply lacks the manpower to be in all places at all times.[1] At the same time, however, the march of technology presents growing difficulties to America's allies and partners in their ability to support this goal. The US is not ignorant of these challenges. The American military, particularly its Joint Forces Command in Norfolk, VA, has devoted a great deal of effort to studying the problem of coalition interoperability. The change in name in 2005 of the annual Joint Warfare Interoperability Demonstration, which highlights new technology that seeks to improve interoperability, to the Coalition Warfare Interoperability Demonstration (CWID) highlighted the seriousness with which the Pentagon views the issue. Nevertheless, the evolution of military technology and doctrine towards information-centric models presents issues that will be difficult to resolve. The problem stems from the fact that the evolution of NCW, as an operational concept devised to create a competitive edge by taking advantage of technological developments at the tactical level, is now driving larger strategic issues in terms of military cooperation between the US and its partners.

Political constraints, imposed by the nature of the international environment and the role played by warfare within it, will ultimately frustrate the technological projects of the United States to keep its alliance partners fully engaged in its security policy. The ultimate result of this development may be increasing unilateralism in US security policy, and a growing reliance on America's partners to play subordinate roles, limited largely to peace support, stability and reconstruction operations. The free flow of information sought by NCW will be critically limited by the impact of international anarchy on state-to-state cooperation. The fact that states have different interests will further hamper cooperation in security endeavours, especially during the period of limited warfare that characterises the current unipolar international environment. Thus, the current global political environment will obstruct the drive to increase levels of interoperability between militaries. As such, prognostications that NCW will represent a new paradigm for military operations will ultimately prove false for those who seek to operate with the US, including its most trusted military allies.

It is well recognised that NCW is changing how militaries operate, both in battle and in 'operations other than war', and that the sharing of information can only grow in importance as armed forces continue their never-ending quest for competitive advantage. It is also axiomatic that the potential for failure in coalition operations exists should partners diverge too greatly in terms of their ability to operate together. There remains hope, however, that technical means may obviate this problem. The search for an 'interoperability black box' continues to attract the United States and its closest allies, and various forums have been established to explore this issue. These concerns are being addressed by the ABCA (Australia, Britain, Canada and America) nations. Seven countries[2] have established the Multinational Interoperability Council (MIC) to explore common concerns. The CWID is also part of this effort. Finally, limited operational experiments have been developed by the J9 organisation of Joint Forces Command and its allied partners, to test evolving concepts of information exchange in operational scenarios.

However, actors in both the technical and policy communities have not yet recognised that the problem they are attempting to resolve may have no answer. Policy barriers hinder allies, even close ones, from sharing information with each other transparently and, consequently, issues of allied and coalition interoperability will not be easily addressed. Indeed, as ICT becomes ever-more important to military operations, the United States may over time find itself able to operate with fewer and fewer partners.

The international environment and military cooperation

How the nature of the international environment and the role states play there will affect the assumptions made by NCW theory about international military cooperation is an unexplored question. The principal reason for this is that analyses of networking have concentrated on the technological issues involved. Moreover, the literature is dominated by American authors writing about American developments and experiences. Allied perspectives have been limited largely to major partners, notably the British, who still have some capacity for independent action and unilateral operations.[3]

As Glenn Snyder points out, 'anarchy is the basic cause of alliances and their Achilles heel'.[4] Security fears create the need for alliances, and yet the same anarchic conditions lead to doubts as to the reliability of any agreement made at the international level. Shared interests and threat perceptions create mutually dependent interstate relationships, but do not necessarily ensure perfect cooperation between partners, even within alliances. As a state can never be certain that its partners will completely fulfil their obligations, each state participates with the goal of minimising its contribution, while maximising its partners' obligations.[5]

The distinguishing characteristic between alliances and coalitions concerns the extent of the shared interests that bring them into being. While coalition partners may share some interests, they do not do so to the same depth or for the same length of time as true alliance partners. Indeed, coalition partners may be competitors in other areas, or may choose to oppose each other even on related issues. A coalition organised around a particular issue thus tends to be driven by the state that possesses the greatest interest in that issue. The level of cooperation it can expect will vary in line with how closely its interests match those of its partners.

In both alliances and coalitions, bargaining over strategic direction and operational tasks assumes the form of placing the alliance or coalition deliberately at risk in order to coerce partners into acquiescence. In military cooperation, the bargaining power of any state is related to its overall dependency on its alliance partners. States that are able to exploit asymmetrical relationships effectively within an alliance will gain greater bargaining power.[6] As Snyder puts it, 'dependency refers to the degree of harm that partners could inflict on each other by terminating the relationship'.[7] Those with a crucial supply of an important asset, be it military or diplomatic resources, will enjoy enhanced bargaining power with their partners. By threatening to deny access to those resources, they are able to manipulate their partners' fear of abandonment to extract concessions from them.[8]

The military dependency of one state on another is powerfully shaped by threat perceptions. Polarity effectively determines the rigidity of military obligations each state owes to its partners. Multipolar environments are marked by high degrees of fluidity between partners, whereas bipolar environments are far more stable.[9] The present unipolar environment has had a distinct impact on how states approach security cooperation. Contemporary coalitions are characterised by the speed of their formation, their tendency to coalesce around issues of peace support and international stability, their lack of a strict hierarchy (and thus the absence of any disciplinary features), and the relative lack of strong national interests guiding their creation (which means that the cost of withdrawing from them is relatively small).[10] This is to be expected when a single state represents the sole guarantor of international order; there is general agreement that existing norms represent all states' best interests, and no competing power is available to impose substantially different ones. As such, in the post-Cold War period we have tended to see far more flexible and temporary 'coalitions of the willing', including among states with formal alliance relationships, as with NATO and the United States in Afghanistan.

Limited war and interoperability

Kenneth Gause of the Center for Naval Analysis is one of the few writers on NCW to recognise that interoperability is not just a question of technology, but one that also concerns the nature of participation:

> For those allies that want to operate closely with the US in prominent positions, even in high threat environments, the level of interoperability will have to be high, possibly bordering on seamless. However, for other allies, the demands of interoperability will be lower.[11]

Still, Gause makes no mention of the role politics may play in shaping decisions on the level of participation. How directly a state is willing to commit itself to any given conflict will have a direct impact on the level of interoperability between partners at all levels of warfare.

Commitments to fight in a particular war or decisions to align with a specific nation are based on strategic rather than operational rationales; alliances made during war differ significantly from those entered into during peacetime. Wartime pacts are made against a particular country or countries, while peacetime pacts are usually less specific.[12] In war, alliances are frequently temporary and are aimed at winning. They are general in nature and comprise the total interests of the parties. In peacetime, however, alliances are more commonly limited to a fraction of the total interests of a state.[13]

Limitations in warfare are generally described in terms of geography (where operations can or cannot take place), objectives (how victory is defined), means (what weapons will be employed), and targeting (whether to engage in counterforce or counter-value strategies).[14] Clausewitz remarked that war naturally tends towards the maximum effort if left unchecked. However, states will not commit forces blindly to a conflict, but instead invest according to the objectives that are sought. As the danger to national survival increases, so too does the willingness to subordinate self-interest to the overall collective effort.[15] In military cooperative ventures, Clausewitz argues that:

> The question is then whether each state is pursuing an inde-pendent interest and has its own independent means of doing so, or whether the interests and forces of most of the allies are subordinate to those of the leader. The more this is the case, the easier will it be to regard all our opponents as a single entity, hence all the easier to concentrate our principal enterprise into one great blow.[16]

If only allies were mercenaries, then the issue of what they would be willing to do in order to achieve the war's objectives would be moot. The 'extreme danger', to use Clausewitz's term, represented by Hitler or the Soviet Union forced a level of cooperation between Western states that was in many ways unprecedented. The slow collapse of the communist threat to the West and the ultimate disappearance of the Soviet Union have caused reverberations within the Western alliance that have yet to resolve themselves. Still, it is readily apparent that the calculation of interest in committing to new political objectives has become more and more blatant within NATO.

The emergence of this 'natural' alliance behaviour will be apparent even in American actions. The original US mantra during the Cold War was most clearly spelled out by the Kennedy administration: America was willing to go anywhere and pay any price. It was the doctrine of automatic, reflexive commitment, of 'strategic coupling' and assured destruction. But in the current unipolar environment, America has moved more cautiously, only reluctantly involving itself in commitments in the Balkans and Africa, or being dragged into conflict by the pace of events, as in the Middle East or Central Asia. Vital interests – 'interests that are worth supporting militarily at the cost that must be paid'[17] – can no longer be simply taken as a given, but must be calculated anew for each confron-tation.

Similarly, the interests of America's traditional allies cannot be taken for granted as they often could be during the Cold War. Maintaining NATO's cohesion has become remarkably more difficult in the post-Cold War environment, with each new American overseas engagement provoking greater questioning from allies. With each new commitment, the ability of the Western alliance to speak with a single voice has declined, and with it NATO's ability to deter its adversaries. This was readily apparent in the wrangling that occurred over Kosovo.[18]

Indeed, who is defined as an 'adversary' has itself become increasingly controversial. In coalitions and alliances, because of different interpretations of the problem or threat, and the uncertainty surrounding allied reliability, these issues have become highly politicised. Differing assessments of risk mean that the very conduct of operations has become charged with political significance, rather than being conducted in the most efficient fashion possible. In other words, in cooperative military endeavours, unless the issue is of pure and immediate survival, politics will always trump strict military necessity.

Unipolarity, NCW and the possibility of seamless interoperability

In many ways, the United States has been successful in finding 'work-around solutions' to the problems of connectivity. While there were significant interoperability problems in the Balkans, some were resolved through the installation of American technology in allied formations.[19] Similarly, the US often devises procedural 'work-arounds' in order to facilitate greater allied cooperation. This has been most evident in the Canadian integration into American carrier battle groups in the Persian Gulf throughout the 1990s,[20] and in the coalition naval operations of the 'war on terror' in the same region since 2001 (discussed in the next chapter). There would seem to be a limit to how far the United States is able or willing to go in attempting to solve some of these connectivity issues, however. This limit is defined first by the demands of information security, and second by the nature of trust between partners.

The search for greater operational freedom is the principle that animates the quest for information access under the NCW concept. In theory, universal access to common databases will lead to shared awareness and thus the harmonisation of operational goals and the elimination of inefficiencies in achieving them. But the animus that underlies alliances, however, is not that of efficiency, but rather that of the political interests stemming from the existence of international anarchy. As such, alliance operations are frequently marked by infighting and competition. NCW might be one tool for alleviating these problems in the hopes of generating a common operating picture or the development of a shared awareness between alliance partners, but the problem is political, not technical.

Information release policies are purposefully inefficient in order to protect the information, the sources used to gain it and the organisations using it from the harm that would result from disclosure to hostile forces: before information can be shared, the 'owner' must be convinced by those desiring the exchange that no harmful effects will follow.[21] Furthermore, because the long-term effect of individual disclosures can be difficult to ascertain, and because the career impact of improper disclosure is so serious, 'commanders often choose stringent release rules to avoid problems'.[22] Thus, information security concerns have dictated separated networks operating at different tempos. As Brigadier-General Gary Salisbury, director of command, control, and communications systems for US European Command, characterised the situation in September 2001:

> How do [combined planners] get these national communication and information needs and fit these into a coalition environment? The bottom line is we are generally operating two different networks at two different security levels. We run our networks at a coalition releaseability level that's basically unclassified.[23]

As Dwight D. Eisenhower remarked, 'Allied Commands depend on mutual confidence'.[24] Like relinquishing command and control, releasing sensitive information is an act of trust between states surpassed only, perhaps, by placing troops under even the limited control of an ally; releasing closely held knowledge places technology, operations and even personnel at risk.[25] 'Trust involves a willingness to be vulnerable and to assume risk. Trust involves some form of dependency.'[26] The nature of the international environment makes trust exceedingly difficult to achieve, even in alliance contexts. Furthermore, military partners generally exploit dependencies in order to enhance their control over alliance policies. Thus, we can expect that, just as nations have always been unwilling to place their troops under the command of other nations, so they will be unwilling to share completely all the information they have: 'As close as … Canadian and British allies are in common interests and objectives, there will always be limits to sharing the most highly classified information with these nations'.[27] In the past, this reluctance did not typically jeopardise operations. However, in NCW information is the cornerstone of all action; the existence of separate networks operating at different speeds will have a serious impact on battle rhythms.

NCW, then, will have an enormous bearing on how alliances and particularly coalitions conduct their operations in the future. The United States is certainly willing to share much of its information with its closest allies, typically the UK, Australia, Canada, and even New Zealand in certain circumstances. However, for the forces of countries not in this privileged club, integration into American networks will be increasingly difficult, depending on how often they operate with US forces and the degree of trust extended to them. Forces not permitted to take part in planning will ultimately be restricted simply to taking orders, and possibly assuming high-casualty or politically distasteful roles.[28] Multinational operations may become more and more circumscribed, and military cooperation, perhaps even with America's most privileged partners, will be accepted only under the most restrictive circumstances. The United States is unlikely to hamstring its own military forces or to slow its implementation of NCW given the perceptible benefits. It may decide simply to forego alliance participation entirely.[29] Information release policy may ultimately decide, not only the shape and nature of coalitions, but also whether they exist at all. Finally, American military primacy will probably place additional barriers in the way of information sharing between states, particularly between the United States and its allies. Armed as it is with the full panoply of information garnered by its worldwide intelligence services, the US will provide more than the lion's share of information to its partners, and will only seek highly specialised intelligence from them. Furthermore, the environment of US military primacy itself will generate increasing distrust among America's partners as the role of independent national interests in shaping policy becomes stronger.

As information becomes more central to modern operations, the shadow of unilateralism will loom heavily. States will continue to share information among themselves, but perfect transparency in the form of seamless interoperability will be impossible. Information is simply too central to the competitive advantages offered by NCW to be jeopardised by automatic disclosure. Such disclosure may happen on a case-by-case basis, depending on the nature of the conflict and the partners with which the US is cooperating. But the dictates of sovereignty will ensure that seamless interoperability will remain confined to the realm of the speculative.

CHAPTER FOUR

Networks in the Coalition Environment

Coalition networks received their first operational tests with the commencement of *Operation Enduring Freedom* in Afghanistan in late 2001. These networks in general worked very well, and helped the US to manage diverse coalition partners with widely varying levels of technical and professional capabilities, as well as political commitment. That said, these were high-end allies. In this respect, the success of operations in Afghanistan masks a broader set of obstacles.

Tactical, operational and strategic issues confronting networked coalitions

Research on coalitions and networks is particularly intense in professional military education programmes. While there are few common themes among these papers, military students, many of them writing on issues they confronted while serving in a variety of coalition operations, are in general agreement that NCW poses a significant threat to coalition operations as the US moves decisively to integrate ICT into its operational concepts.[1] The challenges posed by ICT to coalitions exist at all levels of warfare. For example, many analyses of NCW in a coalition environment suggest that the problem is largely one of poor systems integration, or the result of a general lack of capital investment in particular types of technology.[2] Other authors conflate the issue of coalition interoperability with that of joint-service interoperability.[3] Underlying tactical approaches to the problem is the assumption that the proper adoption of technology and associated doctrine will be sufficient to address the problem of information exchange within coalitions.[4]

Indeed, by 2003 information technology seemed to be increasingly complicating coalition operations, rather than simplifying them. One analysis of CENTCOM operations in Afghanistan and Iraq that year noted that American planners were dealing with more than 84 different coalition networks. Only 26 of these had secure Boundary Protection Services (BPS), the fundamental basis of information security. Needless to say, interoperability between this wide variety of networks was extremely variable, and mostly non-existent. As such, information exchange between members of the coalition was often a sluggish affair.[5]

Some of these problems can be ascribed to technical difficulties in linking networks together. Others can be traced to differences in procedures for issuing and formatting intelligence for dissemination, hampering the process of knowledge management. The most common complaint among coalition partners, however, is in terms of the protocols regulating information release, an issue that affects the tactical, operational and strategic levels alike. As early as 1996, American intelligence officials identified this as an issue that would complicate or jeopardise military collaboration between the US and its partners. For this reason, the Director of Central Intelligence issued a directive ordering specific changes to the handling of intelligence and its sharing with, among others, foreign governments and agencies. DCID1/7 required that intelligence be formatted for easy distribution to all users, including foreign elements cooperating with the US on common security objectives. It argued that caveats and control markings such as NOFORN, WNINTEL, REL TO (releasable to) and REL[6] overly complicated intelligence-sharing, especially since these were usually applied with relatively little assessment as to their necessity. DCID1/7 attempted to resolve these problems by eliminating the various caveats and control markings, and suggesting methods by which even highly sensitive intelligence could be produced that would ultimately be releasable in a coalition environment.[7]

Coalition complaints about the continued application of these caveats persisted long after this new policy was issued.[8] As one study put it, 'it is highly unlikely that raw real time data from strategic sensors would be made available to coalition partners. Rather only track information would be provided.[9] (Track information is processed information from radar returns, showing the 'track' that a target on a radar screen is following, and other information associated with its identity.) Nor did there seem to be a particular technical solution to sort out who received what. At that stage, filtering technology had 'not been designed to differentiate between data releasable to one nation from that releasable to another'.[10] Given the shortage of foreign disclosure officers, and the disparate nature of the coalition cobbled together by the United States to fight the 'war on terror', this problem is unlikely to be solved in the near future. Thus, despite a recognition of the problems intelligence dissemination was causing at the operational level, and a declared need to expand cooperation with America's foreign partners, the demands of national security have continued to frustrate information exchange.[11]

Efforts to network coalition partners

With the introduction of computer networking technology and the benefits associated with it, the United States and its principal allies have established a number of new forums for discussing and resolving the pressing problems of information exchange. The Combined Communications and Electronics Board (CCEB) and the MIC both took on the challenge of improving the principal Western states' capacity to exchange information among themselves.[12] In its *Coalition Network Strategy*, released in June 2004 and updated a year later, the CCEB seeks to move its members away from multiple bilateral network connections and towards a single coalition domain 'supporting information exchange at different security classification and releaseability levels between different coalition partners and communities at all levels of command'.[13] This is an ambitious aim given the problems associated not only with user authentication and information assurance, but also alliance politics. Coalition networks suffer from access problems because of the large numbers of individuals from many different organisations and nationalities that must be linked together. Because of their size and composition, coalition networks tend to be more vulnerable to breakdowns in communication links, suffer from poor confidentiality in terms of their data and are troubled by complex configuration management due to the many different types of computer systems and software applications that must be linked together.[14]

Strategic or national domains permit information sharing within a nation's borders and thus tend to be highly secure, rigidly configured networks that permit little or no access for external partners. Allied or bilateral domains permit a certain degree of sharing between national domains, based as they are on pre-established information-exchange agreements. Many are permanently established networks that 'tunnel' into each other, permitting the exchange of e-mail and sometimes web browsing. Information security is difficult to build into coalition networks because of the often ad hoc way in which coalitions are formed, and the tendency of nations to move in and out of them. Thus, coalition networks are frequently stand-alone systems shared between the various partners.[15]

Given the advantages of networks in general to military forces, higher levels of information security on a network permit greater degrees of shared awareness and collaboration. While all members of the coalition may have access to the 'track information', those that also possess the intelligence that has cued the sensors, the raw data they are generating, and the details of plans under development can make more refined judgements on the nature of that track and the likely actions that may have to be performed. However, such information on coalition networks has occasionally been absent or of dubious quality.

Of course, securing unity of effort has always been the principal challenge confronting coalition commanders. The standard solution for allies has typically been geographical dispersion between forces to obviate the need for complex coordination or to reduce the possibility of friendly-fire incidents. Within a networked environment, information technology should, in theory, ease the challenge presented by getting the militaries of different nations to conduct combined operations effectively. Examining the annual reports of the MIC, however, one senses the frustration among military officers confronting this challenge. In the first report, in 1999, reference was made to 'low-level personnel' making decisions on intelligence sharing that result in major operational effects on coalition actions.[16] The following year, the report noted continuing difficulties in information exchange, and called for the implementation of a series of checks to determine where the problems were. Divisions were also noted between partners, with Australia arguing that the recommendations under discussion were 'not aggressive enough', while the US and the UK argued for caution given the need to control information properly.[17] The following year's report noted the 'continuing challenge to draft disclosure policies that meet a variety of different national disclosure policies and processes in a multinational sharing environment'.[18]

As an interim step, both the MIC and the CCEB have sought to establish standards to move coalition networks towards freer exchange. The CCEB established a two-tier framework for classifying networks and their associated levels of security. Thus, Tier One networks are those with BPS, enabling connections to national command and control systems. Tier Two networks possess no BPS, and thus require a stand-alone coalition network in order to bring partners to at least some level of shared awareness.[19]

Two network structures have been developed that reflect this bifurcation. The Coalition Enterprise Regional Information Exchange System (CENTRIXS) is an operational-level network, supporting regional commanders and their staff at a variety of security levels. CENTRIXS permits the exchange of a common operating picture, e-mail with attachments, a common intelligence picture, web-enabled services, and secure voice links. Currently, CENTRIXS is a family of wide-area networks that evolved from the Coalition Wide Area Network (COWAN) first used in Rim of the Pacific (RIMPAC) exercises in the late 1990s.[20] By the time *Operation Iraqi Freedom* was launched in 2003, the series of COWANs had become CENTRIXS systems. CENTRIXS Four Eyes has replaced COWAN A, networking the US with the UK, Canada and Australia. CENTRIXS Global Coalition Counter-terrorism Task Force replaced COWAN C, and has nearly 60 members. CENTRIXS XX permits information sharing between Australia, Canada, the UK and the US within CENTCOM, while CENTRIXS 0 is a US-only domain.[21] CENTRIXS J permits sharing between the US and Japan during RIMPAC exercises, and CENTRIXS R does the same for the US and South Korea.[22]

CENTRIXS is an operational network; the GRIFFIN system, by contrast, is a secret-level wide-area network that permits collaborative planning at the strategic level of command between the US, the UK, Canada and Australia. As a permanently deployed network, GRIFFIN allows for the proper accreditation of users and the standardisation of applications. As such, it permits information sharing up to the secret level between national domains. Given its permanent nature, a high degree of bandwidth can be employed by the network, allowing rapid and timely access, and posting of information.[23]

Operational use of networks in coalitions: Australia and Canada in the Gulf

These networking technologies were used operationally for the first time in 2001, with the formation of the coalition to fight the 'war on terror'. Both Australia and Canada have participated extensively in this on-going campaign. Although each has adopted different roles in the 'war on terror', and each took very different paths in terms of operations in Iraq (Canada abstained, while Australia has committed forces), each country has fielded relatively similar capabilities in operations in the Middle East. In the naval sphere, both provided task groups composed of frigates for sea-control operations. Australia supplemented its frigate deployments with the periodic deployment of amphibious ships, the landing platform docks (LPDs) *Manoora* and *Kanimbla,* and Canada supplemented its frigates with resupply vessels and the destroyers *Iroquois* and *Athabaskan.* Each navy has a long tradition of interoperability with the US Navy dating back to the Second World War. Both navies have operated alongside the US in the Persian Gulf since the early 1990s.[24]

Canadian naval operations fell under *Operation Apollo*; Australian operations for *Operation Enduring Freedom* were code-named *Slipper,* and those supporting *Operation Iraqi Freedom* were named *Falconer.* Each navy conducted similar missions in separate regions, although Canadian ships occasionally supported Australian operations. Ultimately, the Canadians took control of the 'Leadership Interdiction Operation' (LIO) in the Southern Persian Gulf, the Strait of Hormuz and the Gulf of Oman. The Australian Navy operated in the northern Persian Gulf, where it had patrolled in three separate deployments since 1996.[25] There, it continued to conduct maritime interdiction operations and general sea-control tasks. Despite the similarity between their missions, each navy's operational area was significantly different. The northern Persian Gulf is a shallow body of water, hemmed in on three sides by the Al Faw peninsula, the Arabian Peninsula and Iran. Besides the local knowledge of the area built up over ten years of operations there, the shallow drafts of the LPDs and its *Anzac*-class frigates made the Australian Navy an ideal force to operate in the area. The Canadian Navy worked in a much larger area, first in the Arabian Sea, and later in the Gulf of Oman and the southern Persian Gulf. This is one of the busiest shipping lanes in the world, moving 30% of the world's annual oil shipments. More than 450 vessels transit the area daily. These range from small wooden *dhows* to supertankers, typically generating nearly 6,000 radar contacts on a regular day.[26] Given their different operational environments, the Australian Navy conducted a traditional close blockade of the Iraqi coastline, whereas the Canadian Navy's operations were oriented towards sea control and distant blockade.[27]

The role played by SIPRNET

Ensuring technical interoperability between naval task groups during the Cold War often involved ensuring that the proper cryptographic keys and the right frequencies were coordinated, so that secure radios could communicate with each other. The emerging digital environment has complicated this process considerably because it requires the installation of hardware and software (including the proper version and latest updates), firewalls, accreditation, IP addresses, connectivity paths and processes, and sufficient communications bandwidth to carry the burgeoning traffic exchanged between forces.[28] Furthermore, ensuring that all of this is present has expanded beyond the technical and procedural realm of tactical interoperability and into the realm of strategic policy governing relations between states.

The prime example of the strategic impact networks play has been the growing importance of the US military's SIPRNET for managing information and running global operations. In 2003 former US Fifth Fleet commander Admiral Thomas Zelibor elaborated on his experience with using the SIPRNET in his carrier battle group during the Iraq war, describing it as the evolution of a 'knowledge web' that contained the operational 'ground truth'.[29] COWAN performed analogous functions for the coalition, but one Canadian ship's captain, reflecting on Zelibor's observations, noted that COWAN was 'not where the real battle is being fought, at least not yet, and perhaps never' as it only 'offered a small and sometimes opaque window into the total situational awareness of the USN's battlespace'.[30] Indeed, despite the connections between COWANs and the SIPRNET, many coalition officers continue to express some frustration over the difficulties created by the use of separate national and coalition networks because of the demands of national security. One Australian liaison officer working within CENTCOM described the 'abject failure' encountered in trying to cross-register US SIPRNET user accounts as CENTRIXS X (Australia/UK/US) accounts.[31] Both Australian and Canadian officers remarked on the need for US command oversight, often from the highest levels, so that network interoperability can be made more effective with American ships.[32] The transfer of essential planning information to coalition partners occasionally fell through the electronic cracks between networks as units sought to establish who was responsible for releasing information, or because units, challenged by the pressure of operations, failed to post information quickly enough. In this regard, US military forces naturally operated at higher levels of efficiency because they could look up the information on SIPRNET.[33]

Australia was able to negotiate the installation of a SIPRNET terminal on its LPD *HMAS Manoora* during the autumn of 2002. The terminal was placed in a compartment aboard the ship crewed exclusively by US personnel. Australian Rear-Admiral James Goldrick noted that he 'could not have operated as [the Maritime Interdiction Force] commander without it, so reliant have C2 processes become on SIPRNET e-mail and chat, particularly the latter'.[34] Despite the limited duration and access of the Australians to SIPRNET, the fact that it existed at all weighed heavily in the minds of Canadian officers lacking similar access, concerned that the

Canadian decision not to participate in Iraq had somehow moved them to the outer circle of allies. As one put it:

> the true test of whether or not you were an inner circle member: are you on SIPRNET? ... The only coalition partners that have access to SIPRNET now is [sic] the Brits and the Australians. ... That to me is the dividing line between those on the inner circle with the US. Because the US does all its [operational planning] on the SIPRNET.[35]

'Concentricity' of access

'Circles of access' were reflected in more ways than simply 'network permissions'. Most officers interviewed perceived the US-led coalition as structured in a series of concentric circles of access, with the US at the centre position. The UK occupied the circle closest to the US, followed by other 'anglo-sphere' nations, other NATO states, and then the rest of the coalition.[36] CENTCOM reinforced this structure by insisting on dealing with each coalition member bilaterally, rather than seeing the coalition as a coherent entity. The perception of coalition naval officers serving in the Gulf was that the US did not want to get into a 'NATO-type situation' where everything from strategic policy to operational planning and tactical targeting had to be negotiated in advance. Former commander of the Canadian Joint Task Force South West Asia Brigadier-General Angus Watt noted: 'If you are a coalition member, you plug into the US agenda and if you don't want to follow [it], you ain't a member of the coalition. It's that simple'.[37]

The US was clearly sensitive to any perception that states were not being treated appropriately, and worked hard to ensure that it dealt with each nation in a similar way irrespective of its contribution to the war effort.[38] Nevertheless, the concentric circles of access became increasingly apparent after the Canadian government delayed committing forces to operations in Iraq in late 2002 and early 2003. This contrasted with Australia's willingness to discuss options very early in 2002 (Australia was included in an *Operation Iraqi Freedom* planning cell in October that year).[39] The Canadian military was ultimately able to convince the government in Ottawa to establish a liaison team to discuss possible Canadian participation at the end of November 2002. Following this, 'the Americans appeared to open the doors very wide and gave [Canada] a lot of information about their intentions'. However, as Canada continued to delay its decision, 'the doors weren't closed, but you could feel them closing'. One of the ways this became apparent was in the nature of the information that was provided to Canadian liaison staff. Information within US headquarters is circulated in the form of PowerPoint briefing slides. These briefs are often extremely large, sometimes numbering 1,000 slides or more as each decision point, 'branch' and 'sequel' operation has its own set of hidden and embedded slides. The detail that Canadian officers were allowed to see was progressively restricted until it reached the standard coalition releaseability level, sometimes referred to dismissively as the *Reader's Digest* version.[40]

The physical layout of CENTCOM, both in Florida and Qatar, also reflected this segmentation of information. Outside the Florida headquarters in Tampa is a 'trailer park' of coalition members. This was also reflected in the CENTCOM Forward HQ in Qatar, which maintained a 'Friendly Forces Co-ordination Center' outside the main building, housed in a large inflatable tent. While some coalition members, principally the UK, Australia and Canada, operated as liaison officers and embedded planners within the HQ, all others were restricted to the tent. One Australian liaison officer working at the Qatar HQ claimed, 'physically and in a cognitive sense, I was separated' from the other Australians working in the Co-ordination Center.[41]

Such arrangements within headquarters were not new. Indeed, information within a military headquarters is often controlled even between planners from the same country and service. The physical barriers are replicated electronically, in that it is easy to provide information to the SIPRNET, but much more difficult for coalition partners to get information back out of it. As one Australian liaison officer conducting planning within NAVCENT HQ for *Operation Iraqi Freedom* noted, 'any of the work I would do, would be done on [a] stand alone [system], and then loaded up to the SIPRNET'. Information was downloaded for his work by US officers, and only then passed to him: 'NAVCENT HQ maintained this structure through to execution'.[42] The difficulty coalition members face is that, unless American users cue them to request specific products, the material provided is likely to be of little value, and come too late. In a large coalition, where partners are all requesting information from SIPRNET, the sheer number of requests quickly exceeds the available resources to process them. Those closest to the centre will be best served.

Satellite communications (SATCOMs) and information access

In the Gulf, inadequate SATCOMs created a second crucial bottleneck for NCW. As many as six separate networks could be running on a single ship, including classified and unclassified national networks, a coalition network such as COWAN or CENTRIXS, the GCCS providing operational-level situational awareness, and tactical data links like Link 11 and Link 16. Access to these networks could only be assured through SATCOM channels. Many coalition members failed to provide these channels to their forces, or used 'dial-up' access to commercial communication satellites through INMARSAT, rather than paying for continuously running, leased channels.[43]

In this field, Canada had advantages enjoyed by no other coalition member. Thanks to the towed-array sonar technology it developed during the 1980s, the Canadian Navy has long been involved in the over-the-horizon networking efforts of its US counterpart.[44] In addition, Canada helped to fund the US Navy's fleet SATCOM satellites, and has eight national channels there. By 2001, Canada had also leased 12 continuously running INMARSAT channels, six of which were given to the navy for use in *Operation Apollo*. Each of these channels was further multiplexed,[45] allowing separate networks to run on each channel.[46] This gave Canadian ships a communications capability that rivalled that of some larger American vessels.

At the time, Australian capability was much more restricted. Only the larger LPDs maintained a continuous connection to INMARSAT. The frigates were limited to dial-up access at particular times of the day, or during the execution of operations. The bandwidth of these connections was also significantly smaller than that of Canadian ships, at 64 kilobits per second as opposed to 128 kbps.[47] While the Australian Navy briefly enjoyed the services of SIPRNET, it had to sacrifice one of its two channels on the LPD to gain it as American information security protocols demanded a dedicated channel to carry SIPRNET traffic.[48] Moreover, only the LPD could multiplex its SATCOM connections.

Bandwidth scarcity also affected US ships. While primary units such as the carrier and some cruisers enjoyed larger amounts of bandwidth, the increase in the number of American ships in the Gulf as the war with Iraq drew closer meant increasing competition for a fixed resource.[49] From a coalition perspective, bandwidth scarcity is a serious issue affecting most navies. For example, in the major biannual coalition exercise in Asia, *RIMPAC 2004*, the US Navy managed five separate coalition network domains as well as many national ones.[50] Bandwidth limitations inevitably mean that certain networks, especially coalition ones, will be monitored by American crews less frequently, and given lower priority than the SIPRNET.

Coalition information sharing

Despite the challenges, Canadian and Australian officers described the sharing of information between them and the US as generally satisfactory, and all claimed that they had enough information to conduct their operations. The nature of the threat in some instances dictated the amount of intelligence that was shared (and sometimes the lack of it). Intelligence on the movement of small boats and aircraft, for example, was lacking early in the campaign. Canadian Commodore Drew Robertson, who commanded the defensive screen around American amphibious ships in 2001, was extremely impressed with US willingness to share operational planning details with the Canadian task group: 'we knew what they were doing ... I knew every day when they planned to go to and from the beach, or to and from the various operating areas so that I could organise our ships appropriately'.[51]

Still, the separation of networks also presented problems, especially in terms of operational planning. Robertson's task force lacked both e-mail and voice connectivity with the first amphibious group it escorted as the Americans did not have any COWAN terminals. This meant that US plans could not be shared with the Canadian task force until they had been finalised, and Canadian planning could not begin until the plans had been sent. In the Arabian Sea in 2001 this was a minor annoyance, but Robertson noted that 'in certain situations there won't be time for that kind of wheel spinning ... Those kinds of inefficiencies can lead to real problems'.[52] Later in the campaign, Canadian Commodore Eric Lerhe led an effort to populate COWAN web pages with information to increase the speed and efficiency of coalition force planning at sea. However, time pressures often meant that the US was unable to maintain its COWAN pages effectively as well as its SIPRNET pages. Lerhe concluded that 'the bottom line is we are going to have to, for every operation, pull the levers, kick the tyres, and scream to get everybody working. But people who hang their hopes on [multilevel security], I just don't think they are operating realistically'.[53]

Classification barriers to information release for coalition networks were particularly evident in the interaction between Special Forces and the coalition. Both the Australians and Canadians experienced at least one incident each that nearly resulted in friendly-fire attacks on US Navy SEAL teams. In each case, SEAL teams had failed to keep even their own national forces informed of their activities, leading to widespread confusion as to whether the team involved was a friendly force or an enemy target. Coordination over radio nets between coalition forces ultimately resolved the problem, although in the Australian case not before authority to open fire had already been given.[54] The significance of these events points to the challenge that highly classified networks present to coalition operations should information barriers for more conventional operations come to resemble those currently present on Special Forces networks.

In general, intelligence sharing is conducted on special-access networks between the American, British, Australian and Canadian coalition partners. However, during operations in the Gulf between 2002 and 2003 the quality of some of this material was often uncertain. In terms of the LIO being conducted by the coalition against al-Qaeda, good intelligence on intended routes was often lacking.[55] So-called 'actionable' intelligence was also suspect. As Robertson noted:

> I found it useful that actionable intelligence could lead to nothing because it reminded me and it reminded my COs that actionable intelligence isn't a certainty, it's a probability … You wouldn't want to over-react and find that you had just done harm to some poor merchant mariners of the region.[56]

Even basic track information shared on these networks was often not accepted as accurate. For example, the GCCS is used to manage track information globally. In Lerhe's task force, reservist specialists double-checked GCCS data with information found on port websites. Significant discrepancies between the GCCS data and these open sources led to considerable scepticism of the GCCS system within Lerhe's task force from time to time.[57]

Coalition forces developed a series of databases to track the enormous amounts of shipping passing through the region. These databases were important for three reasons. Firstly, the maritime task forces in the Persian Gulf, the Gulf of Oman and the sea around the Horn of Africa did not possess adequate resources to interpret the data they were collecting properly. Each task force thus shared its database with the others and with NAVCENT HQ, where naval intelligence specialists could 'mine' it for more specific data. Secondly, the sheer number of vessels passing through the region meant that the coalition had to be very selective in terms of which vessels were boarded. Boarding ships that had already been cleared was an obvious waste of resources. Thirdly, these databases helped the coalition to establish the appearance of a professional and competent boarding regime. Convincing ships' masters that boardings did not take place on a whim increased trust in the coalition and led to a higher compliance rate. This was true even for the small boats transporting economic migrants between Pakistan and the Gulf States. When boat captains realised that coalition forces were only interested in determining the presence or absence of terrorist suspects among their passengers, they became much more cooperative.[58]

The sharing regimes that were ultimately established between coalition partners resulted in considerable synchronisation, innovation and self-adaptation, as the theorists of NCW had anticipated. The importance of this self-adaptation became apparent during the naval gunfire missions *HMAS Anzac* conducted with Royal Marine units on the Al Faw peninsula on 21 March 2003. The Royal Navy ship *HMS Chatham* also participated in this mission, but a misfire interrupted its support for the Marines. *Anzac* was able to take over the fire mission it had been following over the network, having already entered all the fire-control data into its own system.[59] The increasingly vital role played by networks in sharing information among partners was summed up by Lerhe, who noted:

> What's your level of tolerance for going into the ops room and saying 'Tell the Italian ship *Euro* to go north and intercept that ship,' … and my guy turning around and telling me 'Sir, we don't have comms with the *Euro.*' … Sure it's extra work, but COWAN is 100%. What's the alternative? Is 96% really the alternative? No! Because Al Qaeda's going to be on the 97th. So it's all or nothing.[60]

The human in the loop: liaison

Given the organisational and electronic challenges of sharing information among coalition partners, the human element was often decisive in making the growing electronic environment effective. Liaison officers, long employed to coordinate coalition operations, played a critical role in ensuring that information gaps did not persist. So vital was this liaison function that the most important members of a task force's team were often sent to ensure proper communications between coalition units.[61] The location of liaison officers within a foreign headquarters was a key consideration for national commanders when deploying them. A liaison officer's value could also be enhanced by the roles they played there. Taking on planning duties within a foreign headquarters reduced the 'burden' of liaison officers on US forces.[62] Recalling information-age sociologist Castell's observation about the varying utility of network nodes, a liaison officer's 'value' was enhanced when they became useful to the Americans as an embedded staff member: 'And so all of [the Australian liaison officers] picked up, to a certain extent, tasks within the headquarters that they were attached to.'[63]

While status as embedded planners also increased the quality of information these officers sent back to their own forces, that information was very much dependent on which aspect of the plan they were allowed to work on. Liaison officers located on the 'fringe' of activities might get a good picture of that fringe, but little else. Moreover, the US command could easily sideline liaison officers if they failed to perform their planning responsibilities adequately, or if their political utility to the US declined. Still, within the large US headquarters, with personnel continuously moving in and out, coalition liaison officers could contribute substantially to the 'corporate knowledge' necessary for an effective operational plan.[64]

Rules of engagement (ROEs): intersection of strategic and operational policies

While coalitions present *operational* problems for the US, they present *strategic* problems for its partners. These states' politicians may fear that they are too closely aligned with American policy, and the need to give America operational control of their forces challenges their sovereignty.[65] As American planning for operations against Iraq intensified during 2002–03, the concern of states opposed to such action, but supportive of American policy in Afghanistan and against terrorism in general, posed both strategic and operational problems.

For coalition partners, the question was how they could continue to support the US in its 'war on terror' while opposing American plans for Iraq. For the US, the question was how to structure the two operations so that neither would suffer because of differences in strategic policy. On the land and in the air, the issue was fairly straightforward as the theatres of operations were widely separated, and there was no possibility of confusion between them. The situation was different at sea. Since late 2001, coalition units had been operating within America's Task Force 50 in support of *Operation Enduring Freedom* in the southern Persian Gulf and the Gulf of Oman, the same area in which *Operation Iraqi Freedom* naval operations would also be taking place. Task Force 50 included both coalition forces conducting counter-terrorist leadership interdiction operations and general sea-control and escort duties, and US Navy Carrier Strike Groups that would conduct air operations over Iraq.[66] The solution was the creation of two separate coalition task forces: one – CTF 150 – supporting Afghan operations and commanded by Europeans, and operating off the Horn of Africa, and the other – CTF 151 – conducting counter-terrorist leadership interdiction operations in the Gulf of Oman, under Canadian command. This permitted a 'clear separation of activities between the overt warfighting of *Operation Iraqi Freedom* and the picture compilation and maritime interdiction of *Operation Enduring Freedom'.*[67]

The creation of CTF 150 and 151 highlights how strategic policy differences within coalitions (here in terms of differing national policies towards the danger Iraq presented to international stability) affected the management of military operations. These manifested themselves in terms of distinctive ROEs, which were ultimately managed by coalition commanders using the networks they had already established. Indeed, ROEs became as critical an issue in the shaping of operations as connectivity and capability.[68] In anticipation of action, coalition commanders created hypothetical scenarios that permitted all parties to explore what they could and could not do in light of their national ROEs, thus enabling the early assignment of tasks and the positioning of forces. This allowed differing ROEs to be 'blended' together, enabling coalition forces to achieve their maximum potential without violating any partner's strategic policy.[69]

While ROEs are critical in all operations, in littoral environments they can pose delicate challenges. The Persian Gulf and the Gulf of Oman are highly complex in terms of their environmental features and political geography, as well as the maritime traffic passing through the region. Maritime borders are disputed, radio communications are difficult at the best of times, linguistic and cultural challenges confront extra-regional forces operating there, and the relatively confined nature of regional waters amplifies the threats posed by submarines, anti-ship missiles and the many small craft operating in the area. According to Lerhe, divergences in ROEs 'meant some nations would not react as robustly as US forces … many contributing nations lacked the ROE that would have allowed them to forcibly board ships or capture terrorist leaders and would only assist in such secondary but important tasks as providing surveillance'.[70] Nevertheless, Canadian commanders still utilised ships with extremely restrictive ROEs. For example, Japanese ships escorting their resupply vessels provided radar data on distant traffic, giving the task force an additional day's warning of approaching targets of interest.[71] The basis for some ROEs was dictated by strategic policies that were unrelated to the Gulf or the conflicts there. Canada's recognition of Iranian territorial waters, limiting the area in which it could operate in hot pursuits, was related to its use of the straight baseline rule for claiming sovereignty over Arctic waters (the same rule that the Iranians use to support their maritime boundary claims).[72]

Despite the complications of differing national strategic policies, networks enabled naval commanders to stay in close operational touch with each other, and also provided opportunities to discuss sensitive issues privately before they became serious operational problems. Private 'chat boxes' were established to 'express private reservations or concerns … *candidly,* while maintaining more public chat circuits that were more disciplined and with many participants for rapid exchange of information'.[73] An excellent example of the networked management of ROE was the case of the Iraqi tug *Proton*. The *Proton* was found at anchor in the southern Persian Gulf on 23 March, two days after the start of *Operation Iraqi Freedom* and the day after Australian forces had discovered a similar vessel loaded with mines in the Khawr Abd Allah. Because mines posed a 'maritime safety' issue, Canadian Commodore Roger Girouard, the commander of CTF 151, felt that he had sufficient authority under his ROE to board the vessel in order to inspect it for the presence of these weapons. No mines were found, though gas masks, atropine injectors and Molotov cocktails were present, and the crew appeared to behave suspiciously. However, none of these factors made the tug a matter for the LIO. Girouard informed NAVCENT HQ of the discoveries made but was told to release the vessel. He found this request 'strange', but complied. Later, NAVCENT requested that the *Proton* be reboarded; Girouard refused on the grounds that to do so would have contradicted his ROE. Two days later, the *Proton* was spotted alongside a barge also suspected of carrying mines. At this point, Canadian ROE permitted a reboarding, again because of the maritime safety issues associated with mining international waters.

As complex as this episode was, the fact that Girouard was a Canadian commanding a Canadian boarding party lent it a degree of simplicity. Had he been distant from the scene and reliant on a boarding party from another country, the situation might have been even more complex. The incident highlighted not only the value of a network permitting all participants to exchange information and to communicate securely, but also the significance of the transition from COWAN to CENTRIXS in the region. Canadian commanders initially resisted the transition as it effectively meant that 49 additional nations would be added to the network, with a resultant decline in the quality of information residing there. However, CENTRIXS also expanded the means by which all coalition ships could communicate securely and reliably over digital links. While less robust in terms of access to classified information, in terms of managing the coalition CENTRIXS was superior to COWAN in linking all the players together.[74]

Networking the coalition: social and digital factors

For coalition naval operations in the Gulf, networks were an important enabler in a very traditional naval mission not unlike the gunboat diplomacy familiar to nineteenth-century naval commanders. While the naval operations in the Gulf in 2002–03 succeeded in that all the missions undertaken were accomplished and no casualties were sustained, the absence of serious opposition raises questions as to how they might have proceeded in a scenario 'more closely envisioned by the proponents of NCW'.[75] As much as networks were critical to the sharing of situational awareness and in mission planning, operations *Apollo* and *Slipper/Falconer* were very different from those envisaged by Garstka and other enthusiasts of NCW. The need for information security ensured that there was no 'seamless architecture'. Indeed, the information-release protocols of every networked participant engineered just the opposite: a proliferation of networks and thus a proliferation in the number of 'seams'. Virtual electronic borders mimic real national boundaries. Moreover, computer networks have not obviated the need for personal interaction. Indeed, the evidence suggests that, in order for computer networks to function as efficiently as possible, social networks need to be established first. While building an electronic network is a relatively simple matter of capital investment and proper training, creating a social network is a much more complicated task.

Building both strategic and professional trust is a timeless challenge. The fear of abandonment that stimulates cooperation at the strategic level works at the operational level as well. National perspectives directly influence operational thinking. Put simply, US commanders need to win; non-US commanders in the coalition want to make a meaningful national contribution, but they also want to minimise their casualties. Under these circumstances, can the US trust an ally or coalition partner to do what is necessary to accomplish a mission, or are these partners simply operational burdens, there merely to show their national flags? The coalition partner's concern is whether it will be allowed to play a meaningful role, and whether the missions planned by the US will be politically acceptable. The need to accommodate a coalition partner's desire for a significant mission (and thus its influence over an operation) has to be carefully balanced against its capacity and willingness to see that mission accomplished effectively. This is essentially a question of trust. As one Australian commander put it: 'To the USN a new … [foreign] command team was a completely unknown quantity. Only through your actions could confidence be built up with you and your team'.[76] Furthermore, even if trust were established between individual commanders, this accomplishment still had to be communicated effectively upwards to higher headquarters, and downwards within planning staffs. In the Gulf, memos clearly articulating what commanders could and could not do were widely distributed among command and planning staff in order to minimise 'second-guessing' during operations. Commanders also met on a regular basis so that their staff could see how well the leadership got along together. Repeatedly, commanders referred to the great traditions of naval operations, frequently invoking the pre-electronic example of Nelson's 'band of brothers' who fought at Trafalgar.[77]

The Persian Gulf's various coalition networks were undoubtedly successful: they created operational and tactical situational awareness, which was shared effectively among partners. However, several caveats apply. High-end coalition partners like Australia, Canada and the UK have sufficient access to, and professional trust within, the US Navy to guarantee their connectivity, and to ensure that other coalition members enjoy relatively similar benefits. In the Gulf of Oman, American trust permitted considerable innovation by the Canadian Navy in developing the coalition network, ensuring continued coalition support for the 'war on terror' even as the coalition was put under strain by the invasion of Iraq. In this instance, a close ally like Canada was available and capable of leading the segmented operation in the Gulf of Oman – a situation which is not necessarily guaranteed in the future. Again, it is doubtful that other nations could have played similar roles as effectively. Had access and professional trust been absent, cooperation would have been crippled from the outset.

CONCLUSION

The nature of warfare is changing in ways that are difficult to anticipate fully. On the one hand, the complexity of high-tech warfare as conducted by the United States is increasing at a rate the rest of the world cannot match. The best that other states can hope for is the pursuit of advances in niche areas of specialisation. At the same time, we are seeing the growing effect of insurgents and terrorists around the world. This is a natural response to the overwhelming superiority that economically advanced states' militaries, especially America's, enjoy in conventional warfare.

Despite this uncertainty, the modernisation plans of the US armed forces are well in place, and are determining how other developed nations approach the practice of war in a manner unprecedented in history. NCW, originally developed to take operational advantage of the concatenation of military sensors developed through the long Cold War, is now influencing Western military thinking. While setbacks in Iraq and Afghanistan may have tempered some of the initial enthusiasm for the strategic impact networks were supposed to have, ICT continues to play significant roles in shaping tactical and operational engagements in both conflicts. If smaller powers wish to have any part in the military operations influencing the current strategic environment, they must seek greater interoperability with America's new military operating system. If they do not do so, they risk becoming irrelevant.

But the obstacles to full engagement in US-led NCW are not only technological. There are major political impediments as well. There is a fundamental disjuncture between the military and the political environment. As Western militaries pursue their visions of digital operations, the political realm remains imbued with an inherently subjective and nuanced nature that fails to translate into a digitised environment. This is most evident in coalition operations. At the heart of every alliance and coalition especially there is a tension between political strategy and military effectiveness. This tension is resolved only through compromises arrived at by hard negotiation. The digital logic of machines cannot recognise such human arrangements.

NCW offers clear advantages to militaries. The speed, precision and reach of networked militaries make them difficult to counter on the battlefield. These advantages come with a clear price, however. The information that makes these forces so deadly must be carefully protected from damage and disclosure. The contemporary 'coalition of the willing' environment means that today's partner will look on from the sidelines tomorrow, and could even oppose a future coalition. In this regard, information release policy is not only an immediate operational concern, but also an issue of longer-term strategic importance. Digital protocols guarding information security can never be as flexible and malleable as human agreements. With an eye on the long term rather than what is immediately expedient, these protocols will always be more robust than the situation might require them to be.

Thus, there is a triangular relationship between NCW, information release policy and coalition strategy. NCW aims for perfectly efficient military operations that alleviate the problems of operational choice in a confusing setting; the price is an environment of trust that permits free creative activity. Coalition strategies seek to increase political legitimacy or military resources; the price is political compromise over the plans of coalition partners. Finally, information security ultimately seeks to guard national security; the price is tight control.

As the case of naval operations in the Persian Gulf demonstrates, networks can be used successfully within coalition environments. Networking technologies were crucial to Australian-led operations in the northern Persian Gulf. Canadian-led operations in the Gulf of Oman used networking technologies to maintain a fragile coalition in a mission that was an important component of the 'war on terror'. The freedom permitted these two coalition partners, however, was decisively dependent on the US Navy's trust in the Australian and Canadian navies. Such cooperation was generated by a particular relationship between trust, security and compromise, specific to a particular time, place and group of participants. These factors will not necessarily be present in other circumstances. Australian defence analyst Alan Ryan has noted that 'operational success in the twenty-first century operations will be the product of orchestrating the combat multiplier effects inherent in multinational forces. To achieve this effect is undoubtedly the acme of skill'.[1] These are words of hope, but they essentially reflect the experience of trusted partners close to the United States, like Australia, Canada and the UK. For more distant security partners, the operational demands of information security will threaten military interoperability, and thus strategic cooperation. In twenty-first century operations, the US armed forces may increasingly act alone.

NOTES

Introduction

1. Vice-Admiral Arthur K. Cebrowski (USN) and John J. Garstka, 'Network Centric Warfare: Its Origins and Future', *Proceedings*, vol. 124, no. 1, January 1998, pp. 28–35.

2. Anon, 'Kernel Definition', *The Linux Information Project*, http://www.bellevuelinux.org/kernel.html.

Chapter One

1. See http://www.globalsecurity.org/military/world/spending.htm.

2. Ann Scott Tyson, 'Military Goals Claim Priority over Diplomacy', *Christian Science Monitor*, vol. 93, no. 231, 24 October, 2001, p. 3; 'In Rumsfeld's Words: Guidelines for Committing Forces', *New York Times*, 14 October, 2002, p. A9.

3. As Victor David Hanson and David B. Ralston have both argued, the creeping standardisation of military practice is nothing new. However, in the past other powers have had several models from which to choose. Japan, for example, modelled its navy on the British example and its army on the German. Presently, all look to the American military for guidance on doctrinal policy and capital investment. Victor David Hanson, *Carnage and Culture: Landmark Battles in the Rise of Western Power* (New York: Doubleday,

2001); David B. Ralston, *Importing the European Army* (Chicago, IL: University of Chicago Press, 1990).

4. Of course, this does not imply that the United States is militarily omnipotent, as the ongoing insurgencies around the world amply demonstrate. But as Hanson points out, where smaller powers challenge the US, they do so in their own lands, and often use technology developed by the United States. These powers have not been able to develop indigenous technology capable of defeating the US, nor are they free to operate in the heartland of North America. Hanson, *Carnage and Culture*, pp. 443, 453. Barry Posen, 'Command of the Commons', *International Security*, vol. 28, no. 1, 2003, pp. 8–9.

5. *Ibid.*

6. *Ibid.*, pp. 17–18.

[7] The first *National Security Strategy*, in 1991, lists a range of 'Interests and Objectives' that the US would pursue 'in concert with its allies'. In the 2002 version, it is noted that the US will 'Strengthen alliances to defeat Global Terrorism and work to prevent attacks against us and our friends'. See http://www.fas.org/man/docs/91805-nss.htm; http://www.whitehouse.gov/nsc/nss3.html.

[8] Kenneth Waltz, 'Globalization and American Power', *The National Interest*, Spring 2000, p. 54.

[9] Robert Jervis, *American Foreign Policy in a New Era* (New York: Routledge, 2005), p. 12.

[10] *Ibid.*, p. 31.

[11] Christopher Layne, 'America as European Hegemon', *The National Interest*, Summer 2003, p. 28.

[12] Raymond Aron, *Peace and War: A Theory of International Relations* (New York: Doubleday, 1966), p. 99.

[13] Joseph Nye, 'Military De-Globalization', *Foreign Policy*, January–February 2001, pp. 82–3.

[14] David Calleo, 'Power, Wealth, and Wisdom: The United States and Europe after Iraq', *The National Interest*, Summer 2003, p. 12.

[15] Layne, 'America as European Hegemon'.

[16] Barton Gellman, 'Pentagon Would Preclude a Rival Superpower', *Washington Post*, 11 March, 1992, p. A1.

[17] *Interview: Dennis Ross*, http://www.pbs.org/wgbh/pages/frontline/shows/iraq/interviews/ross.html.

[18] *Interview: Barton Gellman*, http://www.pbs.org/wgbh/pages/frontline/shows/iraq/interviews/gellman.html.

[19] *Excerpts From 1992 Draft 'Defense Planning Guidance'*, http://www/pbs.org/wgbh/pages/frontline/shows/iraq/etc/wolf.html.

[20] Calleo, 'Power, Wealth, and Wisdom', p. 7.

[21] Excerpts from *Defense Planning Guidance*, draft, 1992.

[22] For example: 'It has taken almost a decade for us to comprehend the true nature of this new threat. Given the goals of rogue states and terrorists, the United States can no longer solely rely on a reactive posture as we have in the past. The inability to deter a potential attacker, the immediacy of today's threats, and the magnitude of potential harm that could be caused by our adversaries' choice of weapons, do not permit that option. We cannot let our enemies strike first … The United States has long maintained the option of preemptive actions to counter a sufficient threat to our national security. The greater the threat, the greater is the risk of inaction – and the more compelling the case for taking anticipatory action to defend ourselves, even if uncertainty remains as to the time and place of the enemy's attack. To forestall or prevent such hostile acts by our adversaries, the United States will, if necessary, act preemptively.' *The National Security Strategy of the United States*, 2002, http://www.whitehouse.gov/nsc/nss5.html.

[23] Quoted in Jervis, *American Foreign Policy*, p. 90.

[24] Hubert Védrine famously described the United States as a 'hyper-power' (*hyper puissance*) during the Clinton administration. Calleo, 'Power, Wealth, and Wisdom', p. 8.

[25] John Shalikashvili, *Joint Vision 2010* (Washington DC: Joint Chiefs of Staff, 1997), p. 25.

[26] Department of Defense, *Transformation Planning Guidance*, April 2003, p. 3.

[27] Paul Wolfowitz, 'Remembering the Future', *The National Interest*, Spring 2000, p. 41.

[28] Robert Kagan and William Kristol, 'The Present Danger', *The National Interest*, Spring 2000, p. 63.

[29] Robert B. Strassler, *The Landmark Thucydides* (New York: The Free Press, 1996), p. 114.

[30] Kishore Mahbubani, 'The Impending Demise of the Postwar System', *Survival*, vol. 47, no. 4, Winter 2005–2006, p. 17.

[31] Walter Russell Mead, *Power Terror and War: American Grand Strategy in a World at Risk* (New York: Alfred A. Knopf, 2004), p. 120.

From a different political perspective, Christopher Layne agrees with this conclusion. 'The damage inflicted on Washington's ties to Europe by the Bush Administration is likely to prove real, lasting, and, at the end of the day, irreparable.' Layne, 'America as European Hegemon', p. 17.

32 Robert E. Osgood, *The Entangling Alliance* (Chicago, IL: University of Chicago Press, 1962), p. vii; Henry Kissinger, *The Troubled Partnership* (New York: McGraw Hill, 1965), p. 5.

33 Ian Clark, *Globalization and Fragmentation: International Relations in the Twentieth Century* (Oxford: Oxford University Press, 1997), p. 1; R. J. Barry Jones, *Globalisation and Interdependence in the International Political Economy: Rhetoric and Reality* (London: Pinter Publishers, 1995), p. 13; Andrew Hurrell, 'Explaining the Resurgence of Regionalism in World Politics', *Review of International Studies*, vol. 21, no. 4, 1995, p. 345.

34 Christopher Coker, *Globalisation and Insecurity in the Twenty-first Century: NATO and the Management of Risk*, Adelphi Paper 345 (London: IISS, 2002), p. 21; Clark, *Globalization and Fragmentation*, p. 18.

35 Coker, *Globalisation and Insecurity*, p. 25; Mary Kaldor, *New and Old Wars: Organised Violence in the Global Era* (Cambridge: Polity Press, 1999), p. 70; M. Singer and A. Wildavsky, *The Real World Order: Zones of Peace/Zones of Turmoil* (Chatham, NJ: Chatham House, 1993), pp. 4, 6; Thomas P. Barnett, *The Pentagon's New Map: War and Peace in the Twenty-First Century* (New York: Berkley Books, 2004).

36 Frank G. Hoffman, 'The New Normalcy', *E-Notes*, http://www.fpri.org/enotes/20060512.americawar.hoffman.newnormalcy.html; Charles C. Krulak, 'The Strategic Corporal: Leadership in the Three Block War', *Marines Magazine*, January 1999.

37 Coker, *Globalisation and Insecurity*, pp. 27–31.

38 Lawrence Freedman, 'The Transatlantic Agenda: Vision and Counter-Vision', *Survival*, vol. 47, no. 4, Winter 2005–2006, p. 20.

39 Ulrich Beck, *Risk Society: Towards a New Modernity* (London: Sage, 1992); Ulrich Beck, *World Risk Society* (Cambridge: Polity Press, 1999); Anthony Giddens, *The Consequences of Modernity* (Cambridge: Polity Press, 1990); J. Franklin (ed.), *The Politics of Risk Society* (Cambridge: Polity Press, 1998); Barbara Adam, Ulrich Beck and Joost van Loon, *Risk Society and Beyond: Critical Issues for Social Theory* (London: Sage, 2000).

40 Coker, *Globalisation and Insecurity*, p. 57; Beck, *Risk Society*, p. 2.

41 Anthony Giddens, *Runaway World: How Globalisation Is Reshaping Our Lives* (London: Profile Books, 1999) p. 26.

42 Beck, *Risk Society*, p. 29.

43 *Ibid.*, p. 13.

44 Scott Lash and Bryan Wynne, 'Forward', in Beck (ed.), *World Risk Society*, p. 4.

45 Beck, *Risk Society*, p. 27.

46 Coker, *Globalisation and Insecurity*, pp. 72–5.

47 Giddens, *Runaway World*, pp. 29–31.

48 Michael Ignatieff, *Virtual War: Kosovo and Beyond* (Toronto: Viking Press, 2000), p. 197.

49 Kathryn Cochrane, 'Kosovo Targeting – A Bureaucratic and Legal Nightmare', *Aerospace Centre Paper 3* (Canberra: Aerospace Development Centre, June 2001), p. 12.

50 Rosemary Foot, 'Introduction', in Rosemary Foot, John Lewis Gaddis and Andrew Hurrell (eds), *Order and Justice in International Relations* (Oxford: Oxford University Press, 2003), p. 1.

51 Lawrence Freedman, 'Strategic Studies and the Problem of Power', in Lawrence Freedman, Paul Hayes and Robert O'Neill (eds), *War, Strategy, and International Politics: Essays in Honour of Sir Michael Howard* (Oxford: Clarendon Press, 1992).

52 Andrew Hurrell, 'Order and Justice in International Relations: What Is At Stake?', in Foot, Gaddis and Hurrell (eds), *Order and Justice in International Relations*, p. 27.

53 Ignatieff, *Virtual War*, p. 201.

54 In mid-2006, the US pledged $116 million at a Sudan donors' conference, the largest contribution of all the delegations present. 'United States Commits $116 Million at Sudan Donors Conference', State Department press release, 19 July 2006, http://www.state.gov/r/pa/prs/ps/2006/69224.htm.

55 Freedman, 'Strategic Studies and the Problem of Power', p. 290.

56 Ignatieff, *Virtual War*, p. 203.

57 Bruce R. Nardulli et al., *Disjointed War: Military Operations in Kosovo, 1999* (Santa Monica, CA: RAND Arroyo Center, 2002), p. 2.

58 William Shawcross, *Allies: The US, Britain, Europe and the War in Iraq* (London: Atlantic Books, 2003), pp. 82–3.

59 Cochrane, 'Kosovo Targeting', p. 13.

60 *Ibid.*, p. 11.

61 Ignatieff, *Virtual War*, pp. 198–200.

62 Freedman, 'Strategic Studies and the Problem of Power', pp. 291–3.

63 Freedman, 'The Transatlantic Agenda', p. 30.

64 Justin Huggler, 'Israelis Trained US Troops in Jenin-Style Urban Warfare', *The Independent*, 29 March 2003.

Chapter Two

1 Department of Defense, *Transformation Planning Guidance*, April 2003, p. 1.

2 Colin S. Gray, *Strategy for Chaos* (London: Frank Cass, 2002), pp. 13–17.

3 Eliot Cohen, 'Change and Transformation in Military Affairs', *Journal of Strategic Studies*, vol. 27, no. 3, September 2004.

4 See Williamson Murray, 'May 1940: Contingency and Fragility of the German RMA', in MacGregor Knox and Williamson Murray (eds), *The Dynamics of Military Revolution, 1300–2050* (Cambridge: Cambridge University Press, 2001); Thomas G. Mahnken, 'Beyond Blitzkreig: Allied Responses to Combined-Arms Armoured Warfare during World War II', in Emily O. Goldman and Leslie C. Eliason (eds), *The Diffusion of Military Technology and Ideas* (Stanford, CA: Stanford University Press, 2003); Williamson Murray, 'Armored Warfare: The British, French, and German Experiences', in Williamson Murray and Allan R. Millet (eds), *Military Innovation in the Interwar Period* (Cambridge: Cambridge University Press, 1996); Barry R. Posen, 'The Battles of 1940', *The Sources of Military Doctrine*, (Ithaca, NY: Cornell University Press, 1984).

5 Cebrowski and Garstka, 'Network Centric Warfare', pp. 28–35.

6 In this respect one need only think of the Battle of Midway. Three-dimensional warfare presents far more complex command and control issues than the traditional naval battleline. Karl Lautenschlager, 'Technology and the Evolution of Naval Warfare', *International Security*, vol. 8, no. 2, 1983.

7 In 1942, Admiral Ernest J. King asked Vannevar Bush of the Office of Scientific Research and Development to examine the possible development of a system of radar relays that would permit ships to share radar information, thus increasing commanders' awareness of the tactical situation. The project later switched to a system of air-based radars, which ultimately saw the development of the first airborne early-warning aircraft in the form of modified Grumman *Avengers* carrying APS-20 radars. Edwin Leigh Armistead, *AWACS and Hawkeyes* (St Paul, MN: MBI Publishing, 2002), pp. 3–7.

8 In 1957, after three years of deliberation, the CANUKUS Naval Data Transmission Working Group ratified the technical standard for data exchange. Originally

named the Tactical International Data Exchange (TIDE, 'good for cleaning up messy tactical pictures'), it later became known as Link 2 (given as 'II' in Roman numerals) in the Royal Navy, which was already using data-sharing technology to distribute tactical information among its ships. As other NATO links became established, Link II became known as 'Link 11'. Norman Friedman, *World Naval Weapons Systems 1997–1998* (Annapolis, MD: Naval Institute Press, 1997), p. 28.

9   Robert Burnett and P. David Marshall, *Web Theory: An Introduction* (London: Routledge, 2003), p. 25; Norbert Weiner, *Cybernetics; Or, Control and Communication in the Animal and the Machine* (New York: Wiley, 1948).

10   Tacticians anticipated that Soviet bombers would mass their aircraft in 'regimental' attacks, launching waves of missiles at naval formations in the hope of overwhelming their defences. In this type of tactical environment, it would no longer be possible to coordinate the defence of a task force through voice reporting, nor could the resources of any single ship defend against such an attack. This meant that the area that had to come under positive control by Western ships and aircraft expanded considerably. Norman Friedman, *The US Maritime Strategy* (London: Jane's Publishing, 1988), pp. 162–64, 174; Scott L. Nicholas, 'Anti-carrier Warfare', in Bruce W. Watson and Susan M. Watson (eds), *The Soviet Navy: Strengths and Liabilities* (Boulder, CO: Westview, 1986), p. 146; Norman Friedman, *US Destroyers Revised Edition*, (Arlington, VA: Naval Institute Press, 2004), pp. 391–2.

11   Jacob Neufeld, George M. Watson Jr and David Chenoweth (eds), *Technology and the Air Force: A Retrospective Assessment* (Washington DC: USAF, 1997).

12   See, for example, Colonel Thomas A. Cardwell (USAF), *Airland Combat: An Organization for Joint Warfare* (Maxwell, AL: Air University Press, 1992), pp. 75–80; the concept of 'Agility', defined as 'the ability of friendly forces to act faster than the enemy' is clearly derived from Colonel John Boyd's OODA loop. Department of the Army, *US Army Field Manual 100-5 Blueprint for the AirLand Battle* (Washington DC: Brassey's (US) Inc., 1991), pp. 16–17.

13   Norman Friedman, *The Fifty Year War: Conflict and Strategy in the Cold War*, (Annapolis, MD: United States Naval Institute Press, 2000), pp. 445–51.

14   Milan Vego, *Operational Warfare* (Newport, RI: Naval War College, 2000), pp. 1–2.

15   Timothy Travers, *The Killing Ground: The British Army, the Western Front, and the Emergence of Modern Warfare, 1900–1918* (London: Allen Unwin, 1987); Murray, 'Armored Warfare'; Jonathan B. A. Bailey, 'The First World War and the Birth of Modern Warfare', in Knox and Murray (eds), *The Dynamics of Military Revolution*; Gray, *Strategy for Chaos*.

16   Bailey, 'The First World War and the Birth of Modern Warfare', p. 132. Emphasis added.

17   Defined by the Department of Defense as: 'The environment, factors, and conditions that must be understood to successfully apply combat power, protect the force, or complete the mission. This includes the air, land, sea, space, and the included enemy and friendly forces; facilities; weather; terrain; the electromagnetic spectrum; and the information environment within the operational areas and areas of interest'. Department of Defense, *Joint Publication 1-02, 'DOD Dictionary of Military and Associated Terms'*, http://www.dtic.mil/doctrine/jel/doddict/data/b/00700.html, as amended 31 August 2005.

18   Admiral William A. Owens, 'The Emerging System of Systems', *Strategic Forum*, no. 63, February 1996.

19   The three books are published by the Command and Control Research Project managed by Evidence Based Research (EBR). While EBR is an independent think tank, the presence of Dr David Alberts speaks to the authority of these works. At

the time, Alberts was Director of Research and Strategic Planning in the Office of the Assistant Secretary of Defense. David S. Alberts, John J. Garstka and Frederick P. Stein, *Network Centric Warfare: Developing and Leveraging Information Superiority*, 2nd edition (Washington DC: Command and Control Research Program, 1999); David S. Alberts, John J. Garstka, Richard E. Hayes and David A. Signori, *Understanding Information Age Warfare* (Washington DC: Command and Control Research Program, 2001); David S. Alberts and Richard E. Hayes, *Power to the Edge: Command and Control in the Information Age* (Washington DC: Command and Control Research Program, 2003).

20 Alvin and Heidi Toffler, *War and Anti-war: Survival at the Dawn of the 21st Century* (Boston, MA: Little, Brown, 1993), p. 80.

21 Alberts et al., *Network Centric Warfare*, p. 54.

22 *Ibid.*, pp. 60–65.

23 *Ibid.*, pp. 71–2.

24 *Ibid.*, p. 41.

25 *Ibid.*, p. 90.

26 Alberts et al., *Understanding Information Age Warfare*, pp. 14–21.

27 *Ibid.*, pp. 12–13.

28 *Ibid.*, pp. 15–18.

29 Department of Defense, *Network Centric Warfare Report to Congress*, July 2001.

30 Alberts et al., *Understanding Information Age Warfare*, p. 26.

31 *Ibid.*, p. 60.

32 Colonel George K. Gramer (USA), 'Optimizing Intelligence Sharing in a Coalition Environment: Why US Operational Commanders Have an Intelligence Dissemination Problem', course paper, Department of Joint Military Operations, US Naval War College, Newport, RI, 17 May 1999, pp. 2–3.

33 Alberts et al., *Understanding Information Age Warfare*, pp. 57–8.

34 *Ibid.*, pp. 12–13. Emphasis added.

35 Alberts and Hayes, *Power to the Edge*, p. 56.

36 *Ibid.*, p. 59.

37 *Ibid.*, pp. 4–5.

38 *Ibid.*, p. 187.

39 Paul Wolfowitz, 'Global Information Grid (GIG) Overarching Policy', *Department of Defense Directive 8100.1*, 19 September 2002, http://www.dtic.mil/whs/directives/corres/html2/d81001x.htm.

40 Committee on Network-Centric Naval Forces, Naval Studies Board, *Network Centric Naval Forces: A Transition Strategy for Enhancing Operational Capabilities* (Washington DC: National Academy Press, 2000), p. 31.

41 Statement by John P. Stenbit before the Committee on Armed Services, United States House of Representatives, Terrorism, Unconventional Threats and Capabilities Subcommittee, 11 February 2004.

42 Robert E. Levin, *The Global Information Grid and Challenges Facing Its Implementation*, GAO 84-858 (Washington DC: Government Accounting Office, July 2004), p. 1.

43 The GIG-BE is a worldwide ground-based fibre-optic network, using IP protocols, to expand the connectivity and interoperability of DOD installations. Six sites achieved initial operating capability on 30 September 2004. 'Global Information Grid (GIG) Bandwidth Expansion (GIG-BE)', http://www.globalsecurity.org/space/systems/gig-be.htm. See also Statement by John P. Stenbit.

44 The TCS comprises space-based and ground-based segments. Space-based segments include the Transformation Satellite and Advanced Polar System satellites, a laser-based SATCOM constellation allowing global IP routing and addressing of information, even in areas with no pre-existing communications infrastructure. The ground-based segment comprises the Joint Tactical Radio System (JTRS), a software-based radio that will be programmable to imitate other types of radios thus enhancing overall communications interoperability within the US military. Able to transmit voice, data and video, it is hoped that JTRS will enable

seamless communication, hypothetically between fighter pilots, soldiers and sailors. See Jefferson Morris and Rich Tuttle, 'Contractors Lining Up To Compete for Transformational Communications Network', *Aerospace Daily*, vol. 207, no. 38, p. 1; Robert E. Levin, *The Global Information Grid*, pp. 11–12; Johnny Kegler, 'Pathways to Enlightenment', *Armada International*, vol. 29, no. 5, October–November 2005, pp. 10–14; Johnathon Karp and Andy Pasztor, 'Pentagon Week: High Tech Has High Risk', *Wall Street Journal*, 2 May 2005, p. B2; 'Transformational Communications Architecture', http://www.globalsecurity.org/space/systems/tca.htm; 'Transformational SATCOM (TSAT) Advanced Wideband System', http://www.globalsecurity.org/space/systems/tsat.htm.

45 NCES are the integrated series of applications that will reside on the GIG permitting the military to access, send, store and protect information. In effect, this will create the software 'nervous system' that will operate the GIG. By establishing IP protocols on the GIG, NCES will enable US forces to forego the typical 'point to point' interfaces between systems, ending duplication of effort and the multiplication of incompatible systems. Levin, *The Global Information Grid*, p. 11; 'Global Information Grid (GIG)', http://www.globalsecurity.org/space/systems/gig.htm.

46 *Network Centric Naval Forces*, p. 3.

47 Committee to Review DOD C4I Plans and Programs, Computer Science and Telecommunications Board, National Research Council, *Realizing the Potential of C4I* (Washington DC: National Research Council, 1999), p. 70.

48 *Ibid.*, p. 27, Alberts et al., *Network Centric Warfare*, pp. 60–65.

49 Cohen, 'Change and Transformation in Military Affairs', p. 395; Alberts and Hayes, *Power to the Edge*, p. 88.

50 General Charles C. Krulak (USMC), 'The Strategic Corporal: Leadership in the Three Block War', *Marines Magazine*, January 1999.

51 Alberts et al., *Network Centric Warfare*, pp. 20–21; *Network Centric Naval Forces*, p. 3.

52 Manuel Castells, 'Informationalism, Networks and the Network Society: A Theoretical Blueprint', in Manuel Castells (ed.), *The Network Society: A Cross-Cultural Perspective* (Cheltenham: Edgar Elgar, 2004), pp. 3, 5–6.

53 Statement by John P. Stenbit.

54 'Global Information Grid (GIG)'. Alberts and Hayes point out in *Power to the Edge* that expanding access to information eliminates 'unnecessary constraints previously needed to deconflict elements of the force in the absence of quality information' (p. 5).

55 *Transformation Planning Guidance*, p. 3; Cohen, 'Change and Transformation in Military Affairs', p. 1.

56 Alberts et al., *Network Centric Warfare*, p. 71.

57 'A process that shapes the changing nature of military competition and cooperation through new combinations and concepts, capabilities, people, and organisations that exploit our nation's advantages, protect against our asymmetric vulnerabilities to sustain our strategic position which helps underpin peace and stability in the world.' *Transformation Planning Guidance*, p. 3.

58 Levin, *The Global Information Grid*, p. 1.

59 Alberts et al., *Network Centric Warfare*, p. 54.

60 *Network Centric Naval Forces*, p. 59.

61 Charlotte Adams, 'Network Centric Rush To Connect', *Aviation Today*, 1 September 2004.

62 *Realizing the Potential of C4I*, p. 135.

63 *Ibid.*, p. 143. See also Duane P. Andrews (chairman), *Report of the Defense Science Board Task Force on Information Warfare Defense* (Washington DC: Defense Science Board, November 1996), pp. 37–45, http://cryptome.org/iwdmain.htm.

64 One is tempted to argue against the possibility of establishing a digital identity. Human beings are essentially analogue entities – unique and discrete. Digital entities, through their ordinal precision

and endlessly replicable nature, mean such a fundamental identification will prove elusive in its very essence.

65 Major Joshua Reitz (USA), *Untangling the Web: Balancing Security, Prosperity, and Freedom in the Information Age*, MDS dissertation (Toronto: Canadian Forces College, May 2005), pp. 11–14.

66 According to the GAO, draft readiness metrics went untested, and organisational policies and procedures for managing information assurance were not fully defined across the DOD. See Robert F. Dacey, *Progress and Challenges to an Effective Defense-wide Information Assurance Program*, GAO-01-307 (Washington DC: GAO, March 2001), p. 4.

67 Levin, *The Global Information Grid*, p. 19.

68 Adams, 'Network Centric Rush to Connect'. Reportedly, JTRS radios would be able to 'firewall' information within transmissions. In this way, information would be double-encrypted in terms of both data and transmission.

69 Wolfowitz, 'Information Assurance', p. 20.

70 Dacey, *Progress and Challenges*, p. 6.

71 As one study examining the impact of networks on naval forces argues: 'Strict controls will be necessary at the connection points between tactical and non-tactical portions of the Naval Command and Information Infrastructure. These controls will ensure that only authorised types of traffic are allowed onto the tactical networks, and hence they will provide continued guarantees that the tactical networks can provide highly reliable, low latency data services. These controls will also aid in providing security boundaries'. *Network Centric Naval Forces*, p. 33.

72 Levin, *The Global Information Grid*, pp. 28–9.

73 Joe Pappalardo, 'Protecting GIG Requires a New Strategy', *National Defence*, October 2005.

74 Hedley Bull, *The Anarchical Society: A Study of Order in World Politics* (London: MacMillan, 1977).

75 This is not strictly true in some parts of Asia, where the state has retained a degree of control over internet communications.

76 Robert Burnett and P. David Marshall, *Web Theory: An Introduction* (London: Routledge, 2003), pp. 32–33; 'Wikipedia Study "Fatally Flawed"', *BBC News*, http://news.bbc.co.uk/2/hi/technology/4840340.stm.

77 Brock Read, 'Can Wikipedia Ever Make the Grade?', *Chronicle of Higher Education*, 27 October 2006, http://chronicle.com/tem/reprint.php?%20id=z6xht2rj60kq msl8tlq5ltqcshc5y93y; see also 'Internet Encyclopaedias Go Head to Head', *Nature*, 15 December 2005, http://www.nature.com/nature/journal/v438/n7070/full/438900a.html.

78 For example http://www.911truth.org, http://www.aliensthetruth.com and http://www.anomalies.net/area51/faq.

79 As Morgenthau puts it: 'Where the insecurity of human existence challenges the wisdom of man, there is the meeting point of fate and freedom, of necessity and chance. Here, then, is the battlefield where man takes up the challenge and joins battle with the forces of nature, his fellow-men's lust for power, and the corruption of his own soul'. Hans Morgenthau, *Scientific Man vs. Power Politics* (Chicago, IL: University of Chicago Press, 1946), p. 223. See also E. H. Carr, *The Twenty Years Crisis 1919–1939* (New York: Harper and Row, 1964), pp. 63–88; Michael Howard, 'Morality and Force in International Politics', in *Studies in War and Peace* (London: Temple Smith, 1970), pp. 235–50.

80 Castells, 'Informationalism, Networks and the Network Society', pp. 17–21.

81 Himanen uses the term Hacker Ethic, although he notes that the negative connotations that come with the term 'hacker' have distorted its original meaning as an informal society of technologically savvy and creative individuals intent on the propagation of truth through the free sharing of information. See Pekka Himanen, 'The Hacker Ethic as the Culture of the Information Age', in Castells (ed.), *The Network Society*, p. 424.

82 *Ibid.*, p. 423.
83 See, for example, http://www.opensource.
org and http://www.linux.org/lininfo/
index.html.
84 See Vincent Moscoe, *The Digital Sublime:
Myth, Power, and Cyberspace* (Cambridge,
MA: MIT Press, 2004).
85 See http://www.opensource.org/advo-
cacy/secrets.php, for example. The limita-
tion on secrecy and knowledge is reached
when many similar products are circulat-
ing performing similar services; at that
point, it is argued, it makes more sense to
open up research in order that products
and services can be improved through
information sharing.
86 As described by Richard Hunter, Open
Source development is guided by 'extraordinary talent, clear vision of the goal, a
deadly enemy, extraordinary tools, and
autonomy and responsibility'. Richard
Hunter, *World Without Secrets: Business,
Crime, and Privacy in the Age of Ubiquitous
Computing* (New York: John Wiley and
Sons, 2002), p. 97. *Auftragstaktik*'s decen-
tralised approach to operations devolves
a significant amount of creative freedom
all down the command hierarchy, even
into the ranks of non-commissioned officers. Robert Leonhard, *The Art of Maneuver:
Maneuver Warfare Theory and AirLand
Battle* (Novato, CA: Presidio Press, 1991),
pp. 50–51.
87 Burnett and Marshall, *Web Theory*, pp.
27–8. A classic example of this problem
is the misinterpretation of sensor data by
CIC operators aboard the *USS Vincennes*
in 1988 during operations in the Persian
Gulf, when a civilian airliner was portrayed by the system as an F-14 fighter

jet. See Marita Turpin and Niek du Plooy,
'Decision-Making Biases and Information
Systems', *Decision Support in an Uncertain
and Complex World: The IFIP TC8/WG8.3
International Conference*, http://vishnu.
sims.monash.edu.au:16080/dss2004/
proceedings/pdf/77_Turpin_Plooy.pdf.
Similar issues can occur with respect to
trust and digital identies.
88 See, for example, Sayaka Kawakami
and Sarah C. McCartney, 'Government
Information Collection: Privacy Year in
Review: Privacy Impact Assessments,
Airline Passenger Pre-Screening, and
Government Data Mining', *I/S: A Journal
of Law and Policy for the Information Society*,
vol. 1, nos 2–3, Spring/Summer 2005, pp.
245–56; Michael J. Sniffen, 'Controversial
Government Data Mining Research
Lives On', 23 February 2004, http://www.
kdnuggets.com/news/2004/n05/20i.html;
Max Blumenthal, 'Data Debase', *American
Prospect*, 19 December 2003, http://www.
prospect.org/webfeatures/2003/12/blu-
menthal-m-12-19.html.
89 Castells, 'Informationalism, Networks
and the Network Society', p. 12.
90 Peter Howard, 'The USN's Designer of
Concepts', *Jane's Defence Weekly*, 3 October
2001.
91 Castells 'Informationalism, Networks and
the Network Society', p. 23.
92 *Ibid.*, p. 29.
93 See, for example, David A. Powner and
Eileen Laurence, *Information Sharing:
The Federal Government Needs to Establish
Policies and Processes for Sharing Terrorism-
Related and Sensitive but Unclassified
Information*, GAO-06-385 (Washington
DC: GAO, March 2006).

Chapter Three

1. Frederick Kagan, 'The Military's Manpower Crisis', *Foreign Affairs*, vol. 85, no. 4, July–August 2006.

2. The seven countries are Australia, Canada, France, Germany, Italy, the United Kingdom and the United States.

3. The exception may be Sweden, which is implementing a mature network-centric system in its own armed forces. Still, Sweden has a long tradition of neutrality and coalition operations do not inform its operational ethos in the way that they do the operations of major NATO partners.

4. Glenn H. Snyder, *Alliance Politics* (Ithaca, NY: Cornell University Press, 1997), p. 17.

5. *Ibid.*, p. 17.

6. Charles W. Kegley Jr. and Gregory A. Raymond, *When Trust Breaks Down: Alliance Norms and World Politics* (Columbia, SC: University of South Carolina, 1990), p. 55.

7. Snyder, *Alliance Politics*, p. 170.

8. Walt, *The Origins of Alliances*, p. 43; Snyder, *Alliance Politics*, p. 171.

9. Kegley and Raymond, *When Trust Breaks Down*, pp. 266–7.

10. Steven Metz, 'The Effect of Technological Asymmetry on Coalition Operations', in Thomas J. Marshall, Phillip Kaiser and Jon Kessmeier (eds), *Problems and Solutions in Future Coalition Operations* (Carlisle, PA: US Army War College Strategic Studies Institute, December 1997), p. 56.

11. Kenneth Gause, 'US Navy Interoperability with Its High-End Allies', unpublished paper, p. 7.

12. Peacetime alliances generally limit themselves to defensive pacts calling for mutual support in case of attack, non-aggression treaties or limited ententes. Kegley and Raymond, *When Trust Breaks Down*, p. 53.

13. Hans. J. Morgenthau, 'Alliances', in Julian R. Friedman, Christopher Bladen and Steven Rosen (eds), *Alliance in International Politics* (Boston, MA: Allyn and Bacon Inc., 1970), p. 84.

14. John Garnett, 'Limited War', in John Baylis, Ken Booth, John Garnett and Phil Williams (eds), *Contemporary Strategy: Theories and Policies* (Beckenham: Croom Helm, 1975), pp. 122–4.

15. Clausewitz, *On War*, p. 603.

16. *Ibid.*, p. 596.

17. Robert E. Osgood, *Alliances and American Foreign Policy* (Baltimore, MD: Johns Hopkins University Press, 1968), p. 5.

18. See especially Ivo Daalder and Michael O'Hanlon, *Winning Ugly* (Washington DC: Brookings, 2001).

19. Nineteen old Joint Operational Tactical System terminals were given to NATO command centres to support the maritime interdiction operation against the former Yugoslavia (*Operation Sharp Guard*), for example. See Eric Francis Germain, 'The Coming Revolution in NATO Maritime Command and Control', *Mitre Technical Papers*, http://www.mitre.org/support/papers/technet97/germain_technet.pdf.

20. Paul T. Mitchell, 'Small Navies and NCW: Is There a Role?', *Naval War College Review*, vol. 61, no. 2, Spring 2003.

21. See Gary McKerow, 'Multilevel Security Networks: An Explanation of the Problem', *SANS Information Security Reading Room*, 5 February 2001, http://www.sans.org/reading_room/white-papers/standards/546.php, p. 2; S. C. Spring et al., 'Information Sharing for Dynamic Coalitions', unpublished paper, Pacific Sierra Research, Arlington, VA, December 2000, pp. 29–34; Colonel Robert Chekan, 'The Future Of Warfare: Clueless Coalitions?', course paper, Canadian Forces College, October 2001, pp. 9–23.

22. Chekan, 'The Future Of Warfare', p. 11.

23. Henry S. Kenyon, 'Alliance Forces Move Toward Unified Data Infrastructure', *Signal*, vol. 56, no. 1, September 2001, p. 21.

24. Quoted in Lieutenant-Commander Thomas Spierto, 'Compromising the Principles of War: Technological Advancements Impact Multinational Military Operations', course paper, Naval

War College, Newport, RI, 5 February 1999, p. 3.

25 See, for example, Robert W. Riscassi, 'Principles for Coalition Warfare', *Joint Forces Quarterly*, no. 1, Summer 1993.

26 Chekan, 'The Future Of Warfare', p. 4.

27 Lieutenant-Colonel William R. Pope, 'US and Coalition Command and Control Interoperability for the Future', thesis, US Army War College, Carlisle, PA, April 2001, p. 6.

28 'General Warns over Digitization Split', *International Defence Review*, 1 January 2002; John Kiszely, 'Achieving High Tempo: New Challenges', *RUSI Journal*, Vol. 144, No.6, December 1999; Edward Smith, 'Network Centric Warfare: What's the Point?', *Naval War College Review*, vol. 54, no. 1, Winter 2001, p. 3; Elias Oxendine IV, 'Managing Knowledge in the Battle Group Theatre Transition Process', student thesis, Naval Postgraduate School, Monterey, CA, September 2000, p. 19.

29 Commander James Carr, 'Network Centric Coalitions: Pull, Pass, or Plug-in?', course paper, Naval War College, Newport, RI, 15 May 1999, pp. 15–16.

Chapter Four

1   Geraghty notes that a cautious co-existence between NCW and coalition operations might ultimately evolve, much like the issue of coalition command authorities that persistently bedevils multinational military operations. However, many are not so sanguine. Pope argues that the potential for failure in these types of operations is growing. Carr describes a 'gaping mismatch' between the demands of operational doctrine and the strategy of operating in coalitions. This mismatch is driving a 'widening interoperability chasm' threatening America's ability to operate within coalitions. Commander Barbara A. Geraghty (USN), 'Will Network Centric Warfare be the Death Knell for Allied/Coalition Operations?', course paper, Department of Joint Military Operations, US Naval War College, Newport, RI, 17 May 1999, p. 15; Lieutenant-Colonel William R. Pope, (USA), 'US and Coalition Command and Control Interoperability for the Future', thesis, US Army War College, Carlisle, PA, April 2001, p. 19; Carr, 'Network Centric Coalitions', p. 19.

2   Captain Robert M. Stuart (USN), 'Network Centric Warfare in Operation Allied Force: Future Promise or Future Peril?', course paper, Department of Joint Military Operations, US Naval War College, Newport, RI, 16 May 2000, p. 15.

3   Major Michael B. Black (USA), 'Coalition Command, Control, Communications, Computer and Intelligence Systems Interoperability: A Necessity or Wishful Thinking?', thesis, US Army Command and General Staff College, Fort Leavenworth, KS, 2 June 2000, p. 66.

4   Major Robert L. Coloumbe (USMC), 'Operational Art and NATO C4I: An Oxymoron?', course paper, Department of Joint Military Operations, US Naval War College, Newport, RI, 5 February 2001, pp. 17–18.

5   Commander J. L. R. Foreman (RN), 'Multinational Information Sharing (MNIS)', unpublished briefing slides, pp. 3–4.

6   These terms are 'classification markings' – a 'documentary form of classification guidance issued by an original classification authority that identifies the elements of information regarding a specific subject that must be classified and establishes the level and duration of classification for each such element'. See Susan Maret, *On Their Own Terms: A Lexicon with an Emphasis on Information-Related Terms Produced by the*

US Federal Government, www.fas.org/sgp/library/maret.pdf, pp. 43–64.

[7] For example, DCID1/7 suggests that material be produced in a 'collateral uncaveated level to the greatest extent possible without diluting the meaning of the intelligence'. Where this is not possible, intelligence reports should use 'tear lines' identifying those items that could not be shared and those that could. See Director of Central Intelligence Directive 1/7, 'Security Controls on the Dissemination of Intelligence Information', 15 June 1996, Sections 7 and 12, http://www.fas.org/irp/offdocs/dcid17m.htm.

[8] 'General Warns over Digitisation Split,'; Kiszely, 'Achieving High Tempo'; Smith, 'Network-Centric Warfare, p. 3; Oxendine, 'Managing Knowledge', p. 19.

[9] It is important to note, however, that where there is a 'need to know', the US will provide limited access to raw SIGINT data. Mark MacIntyre and Sherri Flemming, 'Netcentric Warfare for Dynamic Coalitions: Implications for Secure Interoperability', paper presented at the RTO IST Symposium on 'Information Management Challenges in Achieving Coalition Interoperability', Quebec, 28–30 May 2001, pp. 21–4.

[10] McGovern, *Information Security Requirements for a Coalition Wide Area Network*, masters thesis, Naval Post-Graduate School, Monterrey, CA, June 2001, p. 38. McGovern goes on to note that, given this constraint, information is released at the 'highest level of clearance common to all members'.

[11] At the time of writing, there are reports that the US is permitting access to the SIPRNET to its Australian, British and Canadian partners. It is not clear how extensive this access is. Furthermore, it appears that such access has not been extended to other American coalition partners. See David E. Kaplan and Kevin Whitelaw, 'Remaking US Intelligence', *US News and World Report*, 3 November 2006, http://www.usnews.com/usnews/news/articles/061103/3dni.intro.htm.

[12] 'The Combined Communications and Electronics Board (CCEB) is a five nation joint military communications-electronics (C-E) organisation whose mission is the coordination of any military C-E matter that is referred to it by a member nation. The member nations of the CCEB are Australia, Canada, New Zealand, the United Kingdom and the United States of America. The CCEB Board consists of a senior Command, Control, Communications and Computer (C4) representative from each of the member nations.' 'The Multinational Interoperability Council (MIC) is a multinational, operator-led forum, to identify interoperability issues and articulate actions, which if nationally implemented, would contribute to more effective coalition operations. While initial work focused on resolving information interoperability problems, the scope of the MIC has expanded to cover other strategic and operational issues considered key to coalition operations. The MIC member nations are Australia, Canada, France, Germany, Italy, the United Kingdom, and the United States which are nations most likely to form, lead and/or support coalition operations. New Zealand and NATO Allied Command Transformation (ACT) have official observer status in the MIC. The MIC is composed of senior operations, doctrine, logistics, and C4 staff officers from each of the member nations as well as senior officials from observer nations and organizations.' See http://www.jcs.mil/j6/cceb/ and http://www.jcs.mil/j3/mic. A number of other organisations are devoted to the problems of allied and coalition interoperability, such as ABCA and AUSCANUKUS; there are links to these bodies from these web pages.

[13] CCEB, *A Strategy for Improved Coalition Networking*, June 2005, p. 1, http://www.jcs.mil/j6/cceb/cnsdatedjune05.pdf.

[14] McGovern, *Information Security Requirements*, p. 21.

[15] CCEB, *A Strategy for Improved Coalition Networking*, pp. 1–2.

16 MIC, *Report of the Multinational Interoperability Council, 27–28 October 1999*, 1 March, 2000, p. 10.

17 MIC, *Report on MIC 2000, November 8–9, 2000*, 19 January 2001, p. 10.

18 MIC, *Report on MIC 2002, April 16–18, 2002*, 7 June 2002, p. 9.

19 CCEB, *A Strategy for Improved Coalition Networking*, pp. 2–3.

20 The MIC authorised the establishment of the first COWAN in October 1999 in its efforts to improve collaborative planning activities. The MIC noted: 'The C[O]WAN when fully implemented, will provide an apparently seamless and robust network capability of exchanging and sharing information that is operationally relevant to all coalition partners involved in multi-national operations'. CCEB, *A Strategy for Improved Coalition Networking*, p. 4.

21 Briefing note for Lieutenant-Colonel B. Green, (CF), ABCA, undated, p. 1.

22 Thomas MacIntyre, 'CENTRIXS Improves Communication for RIMPAC 2004', http://www.news.navy.mil, Story Number NNS040707-28, 8 July 2004.

23 *Griffin Key Attributes*, 25 January 2005, http://www.jcs.mil/j6/cceb/griffinkeyat-tributes26jan05.pdf.

24 The Australian Navy maintained frigates in the Persian Gulf and Red Sea throughout the 1990s, supporting the Maritime Interdiction Force enforcing various UN Security Council Resolutions under the rubric of *Operation Damask*. Canada also sent frigates for similar purposes throughout the 1990s under a variety of different operation code names. Starting in 1995, Canadian frigates began to be integrated into US carrier battle groups. Greg Nash and David Stevens, *Australia's Navy in the Gulf* (Silverwater: Topmill, 2006), pp. 36–43; Richard Gimblett, *Operation Apollo* (Ottawa: Magic Light, 2004), pp. 32–7; Mitchell, 'Small Navies and NCW'.

25 Nash and Stevens, *Australia's Navy in the Gulf*, pp. 36–43.

26 Commodore Eric Lerhe (CF) and CPO2 Doug McLeod (CF), 'Canadian Naval Task Groups in Op Apollo', *Maritime Tactical Warfare Bulletin*, 2003, p. 1.

27 James Goldrick notes: 'The battlespace was measured in just a few miles and the time available was minutes rather than hours. We could not afford mistakes'. James Goldrick. 'In Command in the Gulf', *US Naval Institute Proceedings*, vol. 128, no. 12, December 2002. Interview with Rear-Admiral James Goldrick (RAN), Canberra, 30 May 2006.

28 Commander John Bycroft (CF), 'Coalition C4ISTAR Capability AUSCANUKUS', unpublished paper presented to the SMi conference 'Naval C4ISTAR', London, 21 April 2004, p. 4.

29 Rear-Admiral Thomas E. Zelibor (USN), 'FORCEnet is Navy's Future: Information Sharing from Seabed to Space', *Armed Forces Journal*, December 2003, http://www.chinfo.navy.mil/navpalib/.www.rhumblines/rhumblines170.doc.

30 Captain Paul Maddison, (CF) 'The Canadian Navy's Drive for Trust and Technology in Network Centric Coalitions: Riding Comfortably Alongside, or Losing Ground in a Stern Chase?', course paper, Canadian Forces College, 2004, p. 17. Lerhe noted to the author: 'In a large measure I believe his [Maddison's] view is that of an East coast ship that continued to lag the West coast fleets NCW progress. I suspect his ship was thrown in at the last minute into a confusing *Operation Iraqi Freedom* picture where the USN was necessarily rebuilding its networks. Moreover, they were concentrating on Iraq and thus the UK and Australia. During my watch COWAN was where the real battle during *Operation Enduring Freedom* was fought and there is no doubt whatsoever about that ... my situational awareness was likely better than the USN's in this most critical of contact sets'. E-mail from Commodore Eric Lerhe (CF Retd) to the author, 10 August, 2006.

31 'Despite the CFLCC C-5 Planner's best efforts, he could not get through the restrictive administration required to become registered as a SIPRNET CENTRIXS – X user.' Lieutenant–Colonel

Chris Field (ADF), 'An Australian Defence Force Liaison Officer's Observations and Insights from Operation Iraqi Freedom', *Australian Defence Force Journal*, no. 163, November–December 2003, p. 5.

32 Interview with Commodore Peter Jones (RAN), Canberra, 2 June 2006; interview with Commodore Eric Lerhe (CF Retd), Halifax, NS, 30 September 2005.

33 Interview at the Australian Air Power Development Centre, Tuggeranong, Australia, 31 May 2006; interview with Rear-Admiral Drew Robertson (CF), Ottawa, 28 September 2005.

34 Interview with Rear-Admiral James Goldrick (RAN), 30 May 2006.

35 Interview with Major-General Angus Watt (CF), Ottawa, 28 September 2005.

36 Bycroft, 'Coalition C4ISTAR Capability', p. 4; interview with Major-General Angus Watt (CF), Ottawa, 28 September 2005; interview with Lieutenant-Commander Mark DeSmedt (CF), Ottawa, 28 September 2005.

37 Interview with Major-General Angus Watt (CF), 28 September 2005.

38 Interview with Air Commodore Mark Lax (RAAF), Canberra, 31 May 2006; interview with Major-General Angus Watt (CF), 28 September 2005.

39 Interview with Captain Phillip Spedding (RAN), Canberra, 1 June 2006.

40 Interview with Major-General Angus Watt (CF), 28 September 2005.

41 Interview with Captain Phillip Spedding (RAN), 1 June 2006.

42 *Ibid.*

43 Allan English, Richard Gimblett and Howard Coombs, *Beware of Putting the Cart Before the Horse: Network Enabled Operations as a Canadian Approach to Transformation*, DRDC Contract Report CR 2005-212, Toronto, 19 July 2005, p. 13, http://pubs.drdc-rddc.gc.ca/pubdocs/pcow1_e.html.

44 Richard Gimblett, 'Command of Coalition Operations in a Multicultural Environment: A Canadian Naval Niche? The Case Study of Operation Apollo', unpublished paper prepared for the Canadian Forces Leadership Institute, undated.

45 Multiplexing a satellite channel allows several different communication streams to be run on the same channel. Thus, a multiplexed satellite channel might have 70% of its capacity devoted to a national secret-level network, and the remaining 30% devoted to a national unclassified administrative network.

46 Interview with Commodore Eric Lerhe (CF Retd), 30 September 2005.

47 Lieutenant Michael Parker (RAN), 'RAN Exercises', *Journal of the Australian Naval Institute*, no. 115, Summer 2005, p. 30.

48 Interview with Rear-Admiral James Goldrick (RAN), 30 May 2006.

49 The number of satellite channels is dependent on the capacity of communication satellites already in geo-stationary orbit, a resource that cannot be expanded rapidly. Interview with Rear-Admiral James Goldrick (RAN), 30 May 2006; interview with Commodore Peter Jones (RAN), 2 June 2006.

50 These included CENTRIXS, CENTRIXS GFE, CENTRIXS J, CENTRIXS C and CENTRIXS R. English, Gimblett and Coombs, *Beware of Putting the Cart Before the Horse*, p. 15.

51 Interview with Rear-Admiral Drew Robertson (CF), 28 September 2005.

52 *Ibid.*

53 Multilevel security would allow sharing of information on networks between individuals, organisations and nations, all cleared for differing levels of classification. Interview with Commodore Eric Lerhe (CF Retd), 30 September 2005.

54 Interview with Rear-Admiral Drew Robertson (CF), 28 September 2005; interview with Commodore Peter Jones (RAN), 2 June 2006; Lieutenant-Commander Ivan Ingham (RAN), 'Naval Gunfire Support for the Assault of the Al Faw Peninsular', *Journal of the Australian Naval Institute*, no. 109, Winter 2003, p. 36.

55 Interview with Commodore Eric Lerhe (CF Retd), 30 September 2005.

56 Interview with Rear-Admiral Drew Robertson (CF), 28 September 2005.

57 Interview with Commodore Eric Lerhe (CF Retd), 30 September 2005.

58 Interview with Rear-Admiral Drew Robertson (CF), 28 September 2005; interview with Commodore Eric Lerhe (CF Retd), 30 September 2005.

59 Ingham, 'Naval Gunfire Support for the Assault of the Al Faw Peninsular', p. 34.

60 Interview with Commodore Eric Lerhe (CF Retd), 30 September 2005.

61 Captain Jones sent his own chief of staff, somebody 'ugly enough and strong enough to give honest answers to an Adm. and come back and tell me what I was doing was wrong'. Commodore Lerhe noted that 'if it doesn't hurt [in terms of human resources] to send liaison officers, then you are sending either the wrong people, or not enough of them'. Interview with Commodore Peter Jones (RAN), 2 June 2006; interview with Commodore Eric Lerhe (CF Retd), 30 September 2005.

62 Field, 'An Australian Defence Force Liaison Officer's Observations', p. 11.

63 Interview at the Air Power Development Centre, Tuggeranong, 31 May 2006; interview with Captain Phillip Spedding (RAN), 1 June 2006.

64 Ibid.; Field, p. 11.

65 Alan Ryan, 'Australian Army Cooperation with the Land Forces of the United States: Problems of a Junior Partner', Land Warfare Studies Centre Working Paper, no. 121, January 2003, p. 4.

66 Gimblett, Operation Apollo, p. 108.

67 Gimblett, 'Command of Coalition Operations in a Multicultural Environment', p. 13.

68 Interview at the Air Power Development Centre, Tuggeranong, 31 May 2006. Commodore Steve Gilmore noted that,

in the planning of coalition operations, knowledge of a nation's ROE was as important as understanding the capabilities of the type of kit and the professionalism of the crews they sent. Interview with Commodore Steve Gilmore (RAN), Canberra, 2 June 2006.

69 Captain Phil Wisecup and Lieutenant Tom Williams (USN), 'Enduring Freedom: Making Coalition Naval Warfare Work', Proceedings, vol. 128, no. 9, September 2002, p. 55.

70 Commodore Eric Lerhe (CF Retd), 'Multilateralism and Interoperability: Impact on Maritime Capabilities', paper presented to the Centre for Foreign Policy Studies conference 'What Canadian Military and Security Forces in the Future World? A Maritime Perspective', Halifax, NS, 10–12 June 2005, pp. 8–9, http://centreforforeignpolicystudies.dal.ca/pdf/msc2005/msc2005lerhe.pdf.

71 Interview with Commodore Eric Lerhe (CF Retd), 30 September 2006.

72 Ibid.

73 Interview with Rear-Admiral Drew Robertson (CF), 28 September 2005. Similar issues were raised by James Goldrick, Peter Jones and Steve Gilmore in their interviews.

74 Inteview with Commodore Eric Lerhe (CF Retd), 30 September 2005.

75 English, Gimblett and Coombs, Beware of Putting the Cart Before the Horse, p. 14.

76 Interview with Commodore Peter Jones (RAN), 2 June 2006.

77 Interview with Commodore Steve Gilmore (RAN), 2 June 2006; interview with Commodore Peter Jones (RAN), 2 June 2006; Zelibor, 'FORCEnet is Navy's Future'.

Conclusion

1 Ryan, 'Australian Army Cooperation with the Land Forces of the United States', p. 34.

RECENT **ADELPHI PAPERS** INCLUDE:

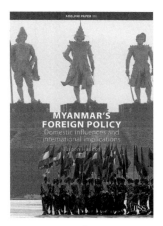

ADELPHI PAPER 381

Myanmar's Foreign Policy

Jürgen Haacke

ISBN 0-415-40726-5

ADELPHI PAPER 382

North Korean Reform

Robert L. Carlin and Joel S. Wit

ISBN 0-415-40725-7

RECENT **ADELPHI PAPERS** INCLUDE:

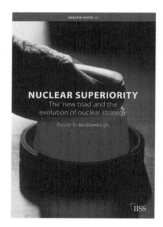

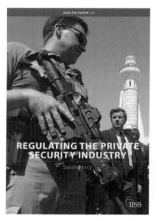

ADELPHI PAPER 383
Nuclear Superiority
David S. McDonough
ISBN 0-415-42734-0

ADELPHI PAPER 384
Regulating the Private Security Industry
Sarah Percy
ISBN 978-0-415-43064-7